Collins

CSEC® CHEMISTRY WORKBOOK

Anne Tindale

Collins

HarperCollins Publishers
1 London Bridge Street
London SE1 9GF

First edition 2015

10 9 8 7 6 5 4 3 2

© HarperCollins *Publishers* Limited 2015

ISBN 978-0-00-811602-6

Collins ® is a registered trademark of HarperCollins Publishers Limited

Chemistry Workbook for CSEC is an independent publication and has not been authorised, sponsored or otherwise approved by **CXC**®.

CSEC® is a registered trade mark of the **Caribbean Examinations Council (CXC)**.

www.collins.co.uk/caribbeanschools

A catalogue record for this book is available from the British Library

Typeset by QBS
Printed in Great Britain by Martins the Printers

All rights reserved. No part of this book may be reproduced, stored in a retrieval system, or transmitted in any form or by any means, electronic, mechanical, photocopying, recording or otherwise, without the prior permission in writing of the Publisher. This book is sold subject to the conditions that it shall not, by way of trade or otherwise, be lent, re-sold, hired out or otherwise circulated without the Publisher's prior consent in any form of binding or cover other than that in which it is published and without a similar condition including this condition being imposed on the subsequent purchaser.

If any copyright holders have been omitted, please contact the Publisher who will make the necessary arrangements at the first opportunity.

Author: Anne Tindale
Illustrators: QBS
Publisher: Elaine Higgleton
Commissioning Editor: Tom Hardy
Project Manager: Sarah Dev-Sherman for QBS
Managing Editor: Sarah Thomas
Editor: Felicity Kendall Hickman
Copy Editor: Estelle Lloyd
Proofreader: Lucy Poddington

Contents List

Section A

A1 States of matter 4
A2 Mixtures and separations 8
A3 Atomic structure 13
A4 Periodic table and periodicity 17
A5 Structure and bonding 21
A6 Mole concept 27
A7 Acids, bases and salts 35
A8 Oxidation–reduction reactions 49
A9 Electrochemistry 54
A10 Rates of reaction 62
A11 Energetics 66

Section B

B1 Sources of hydrocarbon compounds 70
B2 Organic chemistry – an introduction 73
B3 Reactions of carbon compounds 77

Section C

C1 Characteristics of metals 91
C2 Reactivity and extraction of metals 94
C3 Uses of metals 99
C4 Impact of metals on living systems and the environment 101
C5 Non-metals 104
C6 Qualitative analysis 115

Periodic table 121

A1 States of matter

1 a) Kristina wanted to provide evidence that matter is made of particles, so she set up a glass tube as shown below. A white ring formed in the position indicated.

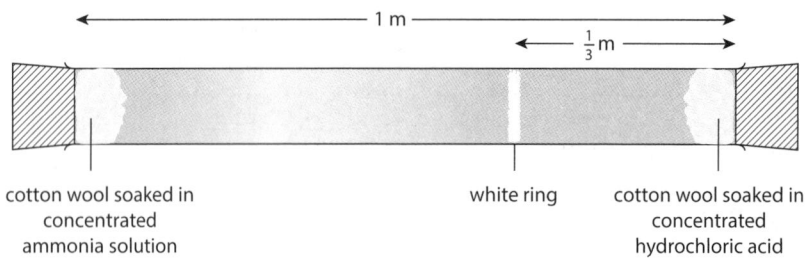

i) Name the compound that makes up the white ring.

_____

[1]

ii) Name the process occurring in the apparatus and give its definition.

Name: _____ Definition: _____

_____

_____

[2]

iii) By referring to particles, explain why the white ring formed.

_____

_____

_____

[3]

b) Paul measured the lengths of two strips of paw-paw and then placed them in a beaker of water as shown in the diagram below.

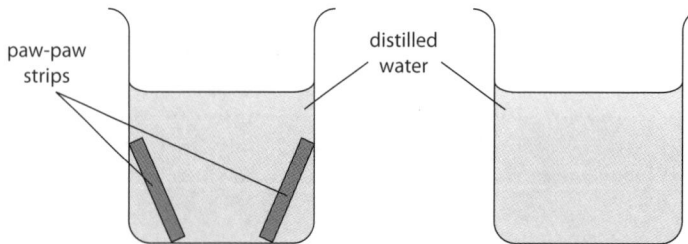

i) In the second beaker, draw how the paw-paw strips would have appeared after Paul had left them in the water for 30 minutes.

[1]

ii) Explain the reason for the change Paul observed in the strips of paw-paw.

_____

_____

_____

_____

[3]

iii) Name the process occurring in the strips. _____

[1]

c) You decide to preserve some fish using sodium chloride. Explain how the sodium chloride works as a preservative.

_____

_____

_____

[2]

2 a) Complete the table on information about the three states of matter.

Property	Solid	Liquid	Gas
Volume	definite		
Arrangement of particles		randomly arranged with small spaces between	
Energy of particles			have large amounts of kinetic energy

[6]

A1 States of matter (cont.)

b) By referring to the particulate theory of matter, explain EACH of the following statements.

   i) Oxygen gas is very easy to compress when pressure is applied.

_____

_____ [1]

   ii) A solid lump of iron has a high density.

_____

_____ [1]

   iii) Nitrogen gas readily takes the shape of the container that it is in.

_____

_____ [2]

c) The diagram below shows how the three states of matter can be changed from one form to another. The letters **A**, **B**, **C** and **D** represent the processes that bring about the changes.

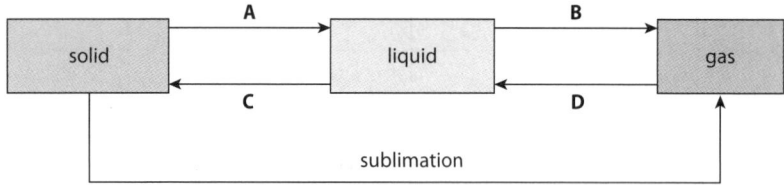

   i) Identify the process taking place at:

     A: _____ B: _____

     C: _____ D: _____ [4]

   ii) Name ONE substance that sublimes.

_____ [1]

6

d) The heating curve for substance **X** is given below. Use this curve to answer the following questions.

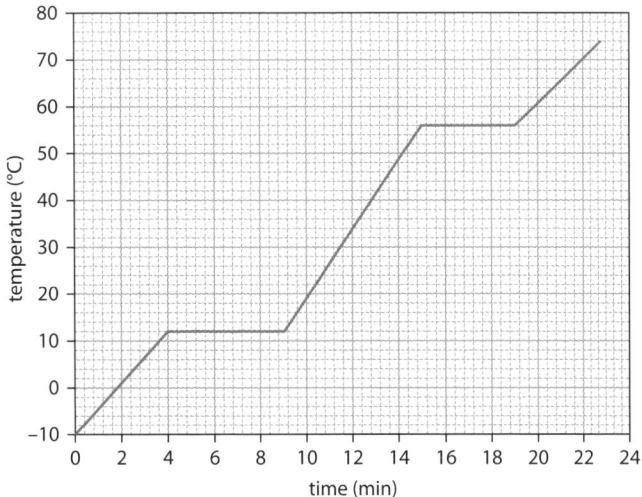

i) In what state does **X** exist at 40 °C?

_____

[1]

ii) What is the boiling point of **X**?

_____

[1]

iii) Using a circle to represent a particle of substance **X**, in the space below, draw nine of these particles to show how they would be arranged in **X** at 5 °C.

[1]

Total Marks _____ / 31

A2 Mixtures and separations

1 a) i) Complete the following table, which compares a pure substance and a mixture.

	Pure substance	Mixture
Composition	fixed and constant	
Properties		

[3]

ii) Distinguish between an element and a compound.

_____

_____

_____

_____

_____

[2]

b) Using EACH of the following properties, give the difference between a suspension and a colloid.

i) particle size

_____

[1]

ii) sedimentation of particles

_____

[1]

iii) passage of light

_____

[1]

c) i) What is a solution?

   _____

   _____
   [1]

   ii) What do you understand by the term 'solubility'?

   _____

   _____
   [1]

d) The graph below shows how the solubility of compound **Z** varies with temperature. Use the graph to answer the following questions.

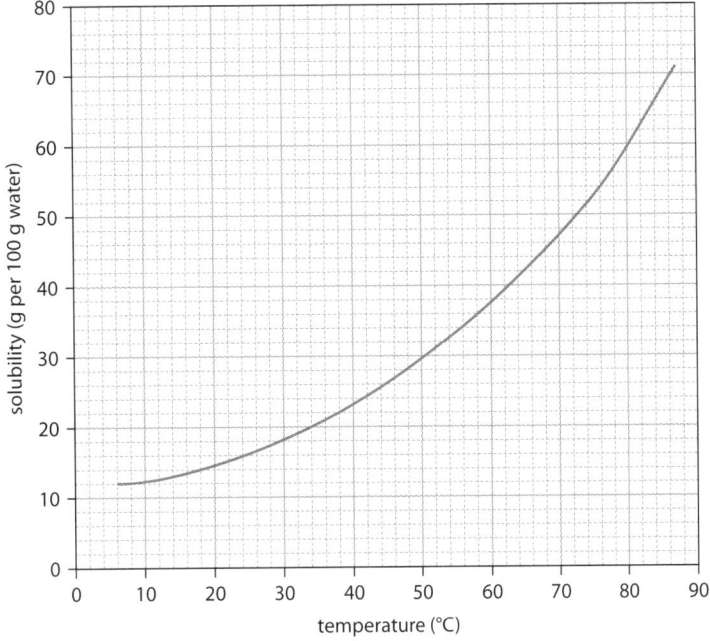

   i) What is the solubility of **Z** at 28 °C?

   _____
   [1]

   ii) At what temperature would 26 g of **Z** saturate 100 g water?

   _____
   [1]

A2 Mixtures and separations (cont.)

iii) What mass of **Z** would crystallise out of a solution containing 100 g of water that is saturated at 76 °C, if the solution is cooled to 10 °C?

[3]

iv) What is the minimum mass of water that would be needed to dissolve 45 g of **Z** at 62 °C?

[2]

v) What mass of **Z** would be required to saturate 350 g of water at 55 °C?

[2]

2 a) You are given a container of sea water, which also contains some sand.

   i) Draw a labelled diagram of the apparatus you would use to remove the sand from the sea water.

[3]

   ii) Name the method you would then use to obtain pure water from the sea water.

[1]

iii) Name the key component of the apparatus used to obtain the pure water in **ii)** above and explain its function.

Name: _____ Function: _____

_____

[2]

b) You are given a second mixture of ethanol and water.

  i) What technique would you use to separate the ethanol from the water?

  _____

  [1]

  ii) Complete the following sentence.

  Ethanol and water are separated based on their different

  _____

  [1]

c) i) What piece of apparatus could you use to separate oil from water?

  _____

  [1]

  ii) What TWO properties do oil and water have that make it possible to separate them using the apparatus you named in **i)** above?

  1. _____

  2. _____

  [2]

d) Joyann, a forensic scientist, has a sample of black ink from a crime scene and she wants to find out whether the ink came from Joe's pen or Sam's pen.

  i) What technique could Joyann use? _____ [1]

  ii) The diagram below shows Joyann's results.

  black ink   Joe's pen   Sam's pen

  Whose pen did the black ink come from? _____ [1]

A2 Mixtures and separations (cont.)

iii) What TWO factors determined how far EACH dye in the inks moved up the paper?

1. _____

2. _____

[2]

3 The flow diagram below shows the main steps in the extraction of sucrose from sugar cane.

cutting and crushing → precipitation → [ ]

[ ] ← crystallisation ← vacuum distillation ←

a) Complete the diagram by filling in the two empty boxes.

[2]

b) What is added to the juice to cause precipitation in the second step?

_____

[1]

c) What happens during vacuum distillation?

_____

_____

_____

_____

[2]

Total Marks _____ / 39

A3 Atomic structure

1 a) Define EACH of the following:

i) atom

_____

_____ [1]

ii) mass number

_____

_____ [1]

iii) atomic number

_____

_____ [1]

iv) relative atomic mass

_____

_____ [1]

b) Complete the following table, which gives information about the three subatomic particles in an atom.

Particle	Relative mass	Relative charge	Location in the atom
proton	1		
electron		−1	
		0	

[7]

A3 Atomic structure (cont.)

c) This nuclear notation can be used to represent an atom:
State what EACH letter represents.

$^A_B X$

A: _____

B: _____

X: _____

[3]

d) Using the nuclear notations given, fill in the spaces in the table below.

Nuclear notation	$^{31}_{15}P$	$^{65}_{30}Zn$	$^{207}_{82}Pb$	$^{108}_{47}Ag$
Name of element				
Number of protons				
Number of neutrons				
Number of electrons				

[4]

2 a) Complete the following table, which gives information about three elements.

Element	Potassium	Nitrogen	Chlorine
Atomic symbol			
Mass number	39		
Atomic number			
Number of protons			17
Number of electrons	19		
Number of neutrons		7	18
Electronic configuration		2,5	

[5]

b) Write the electronic configuration of each of the following atoms.

$^{40}_{20}Ar$ _____

$^{12}_{6}C$ _____

$^{7}_{3}$Li _____

$^{32}_{16}$S _____

[4]

c) The atomic numbers of helium, aluminium and oxygen are 2, 13 and 8 respectively. Complete the shell diagrams below to show the electronic configuration of EACH atom.

[3]

d) Draw a shell diagram to show the structure of one atom of EACH of the following elements. In EACH case identify the element below its nuclear notation.

i) $^{40}_{20}$Ca   ii) $^{19}_{9}$F   iii) $^{28}_{14}$Si

$^{40}_{20}$Ca _____ $^{19}_{9}$F _____ $^{28}_{14}$Si _____

[6]

3 a) i) Define the term 'isotopy'.

_____

_____

[1]

ii) Naturally occurring element **Y** consists of 85% $^{23}_{11}$Y and 15% $^{25}_{11}$Y. Give the number of protons, neutrons and electrons in EACH isotope of element **Y**.

$^{23}_{11}$Y _____

$^{25}_{11}$Y _____

[2]

A3 Atomic structure (cont.)

iii) Determine the average mass number of naturally occurring element **Y**.

[1]

iv) Explain why the two isotopes of element **Y** have the same chemical properties.

[1]

v) The two isotopes of element **Y** have slightly different physical properties. Identify, with a reason, ONE physical property that would be different in the two isotopes.

[1]

b) i) What is a radioactive isotope?

[1]

ii) Outline how radioactive cobalt-60 is used to treat cancer.

[2]

iii) List THREE other uses of radioactive isotopes and name a suitable radioactive isotope for EACH use.

1.

2.

3.

[3]

Total Marks _____ / 48

A4 Periodic table and periodicity

1 a) i) Outline how Döbereiner and Mendeleev contributed to the development of the periodic table.

Döbereiner

_____

_____

_____

_____

Mendeleev

_____

_____

_____

_____

[4]

ii) How are the elements in the modern periodic table arranged?

_____

_____

[2]

b) i) What is the link between the electronic configuration of an atom and its group number in the periodic table?

_____

_____

[1]

ii) What is the link between the electronic configuration of an atom and its period number in the periodic table?

_____

_____

[1]

A4 Periodic table and periodicity (cont.)

iii) A potassium atom has one valence electron and four occupied electron shells. Give the group number and period number of potassium in the periodic table.

_____

[2]

iv) Phosphorus is in Group V and Period 3 of the periodic table. Using this information, give the electronic configuration of a phosphorus atom.

_____

[1]

2 Below is an outline of part of the periodic table with magnesium [Mg], silicon [Si] and bromine [Br] in their correct positions. Letters represent the positions of four other elements. When answering the following questions, use these letters as the symbols of the elements. You are not expected to identify the elements.

	I	II		III	IV	V	VI	VII	0
1									
2									
3	G	Mg			Si			D	
4		A						Br	
5								E	

a) i) Give the symbols of TWO elements that are in the same group.

_____

[1]

ii) Element **W** has an electronic configuration of 2,8,6. Place **W** in its correct position in the table above. [1]

iii) Give the electronic configuration of **Si** and name the element.

Electronic configuration: _____ Name: _____

[2]

b) i) Both magnesium and **A** react with water. Which element would you expect to react more vigorously? Provide an explanation for your answer.

Element: _____ Explanation: _____

_____

_____

[3]

ii) Write a balanced chemical equation for the reaction between magnesium and water.

_____

[2]

iii) Apart from its reaction with water, state TWO other reactions that are typical of **A**.

_____

[2]

c) i) Name the family of elements to which **D**, bromine and **E** belong.

_____

[1]

ii) In what state would you expect element **D** to exist at room temperature?

_____

[1]

iii) Which element, bromine or **E**, would you expect to have a greater strength of oxidising power? Explain your answer.

Element: _____ Explanation: _____

_____

_____

_____

[3]

iv) Why does the solution turn orange-brown when chlorine gas is bubbled into aqueous potassium bromide? Support your answer with a balanced chemical equation.

_____

_____

_____

Equation: _____

[3]

A4 Periodic table and periodicity (cont.)

d) i) Elements **G** and **D** are both in Period 3. What can you deduce about the electronic structure of their atoms?

_____
[1]

ii) Draw lines to show how EACH element shown in Period 3 would be classified.

D

G   metal

Mg   semi-metal

Si   non-metal

[2]

iii) State THREE ways in which magnesium and **D** differ in their physical properties.

1. _____

2. _____

3. _____
[3]

iv) Both **G** and magnesium react with hydrochloric acid. Which element would you expect to react more vigorously? Provide an explanation for your answer.

Element: _____ Explanation: _____

_____

_____
[3]

v) Write a balanced chemical equation for the reaction between magnesium and hydrochloric acid.

_____

_____
[2]

Total Marks _____ / 41

A5 Structure and bonding

1 a) i) Why do atoms of elements bond with each other?

_____

[1]

ii) Two types of chemical bonding are ionic bonding and covalent bonding. Outline what happens during:

ionic bonding _____

_____

covalent bonding _____

_____

[2]

b) Complete the following table.

Name of compound	Formula of compound	Type of bonding in the compound
ethane	C_2H_6	
sodium oxide	Na_2O	
magnesium nitride	Mg_3N_2	
sulfur dioxide	SO_2	
calcium chloride	$CaCl_2$	
trifluoromethane	CHF_3	

[3]

c) i) When beryllium bonds with chlorine to form beryllium chloride each beryllium atom loses its two valence electrons. Complete the diagram to show what a beryllium atom forms and name this on the line provided.

+ 2 electrons

----

[3]

21

A5 Structure and bonding (cont.)

ii) Complete the dot-and-cross diagram to show how the ionic compound lithium sulfide is formed. [atomic numbers: lithium = 3, sulfur = 16]

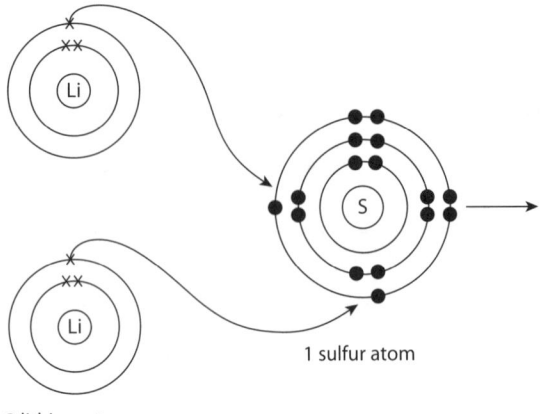

2 lithium atoms   1 sulfur atom

[2]

iii) Draw a dot-and-cross diagram to show how the covalent compound ammonia is formed from nitrogen and hydrogen. [atomic numbers: nitrogen = 7, hydrogen = 1]

[2]

iv) Draw a dot-and-cross diagram to show how magnesium fluoride is formed. [atomic numbers: magnesium = 12, fluorine = 9]

[3]

d) This is an ethene molecule.

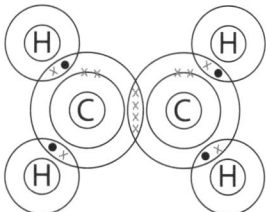

i) Use the diagram to help you write the molecular formula of ethene.

_____

[1]

ii) How many single covalent bonds are there in the ethene molecule?

_____

[1]

iii) How many double covalent bonds are there in the ethene molecule?

_____

[1]

iv) In the space below, give the structural formula of the ethene molecule.

[1]

2 a) The following table gives the atomic numbers of pairs of elements that can bond to form compounds. Complete the table.

Atomic number		Type of bonding in the compound
Element 1	Element 2	
17	8	
13	16	
20	7	
15	9	

[4]

b) A compound can be formed between element **W**, which is found in Group V, Period 3 of the periodic table, and element **X**, which is found in Group VII, Period 2.

i) What type of bonding would be present in the compound?

_____

[1]

A5 Structure and bonding (cont.)

ii) Using a dot-and-cross diagram that shows valence electrons only, show how W and X bond to form a compound. [Use the letters W and X as symbols for the elements. You are not expected to identify them.]

[3]

c) Complete the following table.

Entity	Formula	Entity	Formula
potassium ion		water molecule	
sulfate ion		sulfur trioxide molecule	
hydrogen carbonate ion		carbon monoxide molecule	
magnesium ion		calcium hydrogen sulfate	
nitrate ion		sodium nitride	
iron(III) ion		ammonium phosphate	
fluoride ion		copper(II) nitrite	
carbon disulfide molecule		silver sulfide	
chlorine molecule		aluminium carbonate	
nitrogen dioxide molecule		zinc hydroxide	

[5]

3 a) Describe the bonding you would expect to find in a coin made out of copper.

___

___

___

___

[3]

b) Explain EACH of the following statements.

   i) Copper is a good conductor of electricity. _____

   _____ [1]

   ii) Copper can be easily drawn out into wires. _____

   _____ [1]

   iii) Copper has a fairly high melting point. _____

   _____ [1]

4 a) Complete the following table to compare an ionic solid and a simple molecular solid.

Property	Ionic solid	Simple molecular solid
Structure		
Melting point		
Solubility		
Electrical conductivity		

[8]

b) Explain the electrical conductivity of sodium chloride. _____

_____

_____

[2]

25

A5 Structure and bonding (cont.)

c) The diagram below represents part of the sodium chloride crystal lattice with one sodium ion shown. Complete the diagram by using the following symbols:

- ● to represent a sodium ion
- ○ to represent a chloride ion.

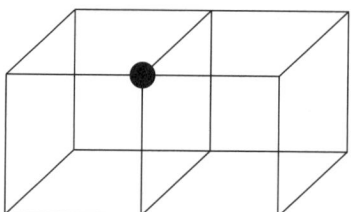

[2]

d) i) Define the term 'allotropy'. _____

_____

[1]

ii) Explain why diamond and graphite have the same chemical properties but different physical properties.

_____

_____

[2]

iii) By referring to the bonding in diamond and graphite, explain the statements.

Diamond has a very high melting point. _____

_____ [2]

Graphite conducts electricity. _____

_____ [2]

Diamond is used in the tips of cutting tools. _____

_____ [2]

Graphite is used as a solid lubricant. _____

_____ [2]

Total Marks _____ / 62

A6 Mole concept

Use the periodic table at the back of the book to find the relative atomic masses required to answer questions in this unit.

1 a) i) Define the term 'mole'. _____

_____

[1]

ii) Distinguish between relative mass and molar mass.

_____

_____

_____

[2]

iii) Determine the relative molecular mass of the following substances.

chlorine (Cl_2)

_____

nitrogen dioxide (NO_2)

_____

hydrogen sulfide (H_2S)

_____

[3]

iv) Determine the relative formula mass of the following substances.

aluminium oxide (Al_2O_3)

_____

ammonium sulfate ((NH_4)$_2SO_4$)

_____

calcium hydrogen carbonate ($Ca(HCO_3)_2$)

_____

[3]

A6 Mole concept (cont.)

v) Determine the molar mass of the following substances.

magnesium nitrate ($Mg(NO_3)_2$)

_____

sucrose ($C_{12}H_{22}O_{11}$)

_____

[2]

b) i) Determine the mass of 0·4 mol of zinc hydroxide ($Zn(OH)_2$).

[2]

ii) How many moles are in 8·28 g of potassium carbonate (K_2CO_3)?

[2]

iii) How many carbon dioxide molecules are in 11·0 g of carbon dioxide (CO_2)?

[3]

c) Determine the percentage, by mass, of oxygen in aluminium carbonate ($Al_2(CO_3)_3$).

[3]

2 a) i) State Avogadro's Law.

_____

_____
[1]

  ii) What is the volume of 1 mol of nitrogen at:

  room temperature and pressure (rtp)? _____

  standard temperature and pressure (stp)? _____
[2]

b) i) How many moles of sulfur dioxide would be present in 3·36 dm³ of the gas at stp?

[1]

  ii) What volume would be occupied by 0·075 mol of oxygen at rtp?

[1]

  iii) Determine the mass of 1792 cm³ of ammonia (NH_3) at stp.

[3]

  iv) A jar of hydrogen contains $4·8 \times 10^{22}$ hydrogen molecules. Determine the volume of the jar at rtp.

[2]

A6 Mole concept (cont.)

3 a) Write a balanced chemical equation for EACH of the following reactions:

   i) the reaction between calcium and hydrochloric acid (HCl(aq)) to form calcium chloride and hydrogen

   _____

   [2]

   ii) zinc hydrogen carbonate reacting with nitric acid (HNO$_3$(aq)) to form zinc nitrate, carbon dioxide and water

   _____

   [2]

   iii) the reaction between aluminium and chlorine gas to make aluminium chloride

   _____

   [2]

   iv) the reaction occurring when chlorine gas is bubbled into aqueous potassium iodide, which forms potassium chloride and iodine

   _____

   [2]

   v) the formation of copper(II) oxide, nitrogen dioxide and oxygen when copper(II) nitrate is heated

   _____

   [2]

b) Write the ionic equation for EACH of the following reactions.

   i) Pb(NO$_3$)$_2$(aq) + 2NaCl(aq) $\longrightarrow$ PbCl$_2$(s) + 2NaNO$_3$(aq)

   _____

   [2]

   ii) KOH(aq) + HNO$_3$(aq) $\longrightarrow$ KNO$_3$(aq) + H$_2$O(l)

   _____

   [2]

iii) Mg(s) + 2HCl(aq) ⟶ MgCl₂(aq) + H₂(g)

_____

[2]

iv) aqueous aluminium nitrate reacting with aqueous sodium hydroxide to form insoluble aluminium hydroxide and soluble sodium nitrate

_____

[2]

4 a) State the Law of Conservation of Matter.

_____

_____

[1]

b) Jamal has only 11·2 g of potassium hydroxide and wants to know what mass of potassium sulfate he could produce if he reacts this with excess sulfuric acid, according to the following equation:

$$2KOH(aq) + H_2SO_4(aq) \longrightarrow K_2SO_4(aq) + 2H_2O(l)$$

i) How many moles of potassium hydroxide does Jamal have?

[2]

ii) How many moles of potassium sulfate would Jamal be able to produce?

[1]

iii) What mass of potassium sulfate could Jamal produce?

[2]

c) What mass of lead(II) chloride would be produced when a solution containing 0·3 mol of sodium chloride is mixed with a solution containing excess lead(II) nitrate? The equation for this reaction is:

$$Pb(NO_3)_2(aq) + 2NaCl(aq) \longrightarrow PbCl_2(s) + 2NaNO_3(aq)$$

[3]

31

A6 Mole concept (cont.)

d) What volume of carbon dioxide, measured at stp, would be produced if 3·65 g of magnesium hydrogen carbonate reacts with excess nitric acid, as below:

$$Mg(HCO_3)_2(s) + 2HNO_3(aq) \longrightarrow Mg(NO_3)_2(aq) + 2CO_2(g) + 2H_2O(l)$$

[4]

e) Under the right conditions, hydrogen reacts with oxygen as below:

$$2H_2(g) + O_2(g) \longrightarrow 2H_2O(g)$$

What volume of oxygen would be required to produce 960 cm³ of steam when it reacts with excess hydrogen, both volumes being measured at rtp?

[3]

f) What mass of iron(III) hydroxide could be produced when a solution of sodium hydroxide containing 12·75 g of hydroxide ions reacts with a solution containing excess Fe^{3+} ions according to the following equation?

$$Fe^{3+}(aq) + 3OH^-(aq) \longrightarrow Fe(OH)_3(s)$$

[5]

5 a) i) What does the term 'molar concentration' mean?

_____

_____

[1]

ii) Define the term 'standard solution'.

_____

[1]

iii) Brianna wants to prepare 1 dm³ of potassium hydroxide solution of concentration 5·6 g dm⁻³. Outline how she would prepare this solution in the laboratory.

_____

_____

_____

_____

_____

_____

[4]

b) i) What mass of sodium carbonate would be required to prepare 250 cm³ of sodium carbonate solution with a molar concentration of 0·24 mol dm⁻³?

[3]

A6 Mole concept (cont.)

ii) Determine the molar concentration of a solution of ammonium sulfate containing 6·6 g of ammonium sulfate in 400 cm³ of solution.

[3]

iii) How many moles of sulfuric acid (H_2SO_4) are present in 200 cm³ of solution that has a mass concentration of 78·4 g dm^{-3}?

[3]

iv) Tremaine has 12·0 g of sodium hydroxide and wishes to make a solution of concentration 0·75 mol dm^{-3}. What volume of solution would he be able to make?

[3]

Total Marks .... / 88

A7 Acids, bases and salts

1 a) i) Complete the following sentence.

All acids contain _____ ions and all alkalis contain _____ ions. **[2]**

ii) Explain why acids can be defined as proton donors and bases as proton acceptors.

_____

_____

_____

_____

[3]

iii) Support your answer to **ii)** above by referring to the reaction between sodium hydroxide and hydrochloric acid.

_____

_____

[2]

iv) What is the relationship between a base and an alkali?

_____

[1]

b) i) The pH scale measures the strength of acids and alkalis. Draw a line to match EACH acid or alkali with its most likely pH value.

sodium hydroxide solution	pH 1
hydrochloric acid	pH 4
aqueous ammonia	pH 11
ethanoic acid	pH 14

[4]

35

A7 Acids, bases and salts (cont.)

ii) Why is sulfuric acid classified as a strong acid and ethanoic acid classified as a weak acid?

_____

_____

_____

[2]

2 a) The diagram below shows what Nicholas observed when he placed a piece of magnesium ribbon into some dilute sulfuric acid in a test tube.

magnesium ribbon
dilute sulfuric acid

i) Suggest the identity of the gas in the bubbles.

_____

[1]

ii) What test could Nicholas use to confirm the identity of the gas?

_____

_____

[1]

iii) Write a balanced chemical equation for the reaction occurring in the test tube.

_____

[1]

iv) Write an ionic equation for the reaction occurring in the test tube.

_____

[1]

b) Write a balanced chemical equation for EACH of the following acid reactions.

i) the reaction between copper(II) carbonate and nitric acid

_____

[2]

ii) zinc hydroxide reacting with hydrochloric acid

_____

[2]

iii) the reaction between aluminium oxide and sulfuric acid

_____

[2]

iv) the reaction between calcium hydrogen carbonate and hydrochloric acid

_____

[2]

c) Write ionic equations for the following reactions.

i) sodium hydroxide reacting with hydrochloric acid

_____

[1]

ii) the reaction between potassium carbonate and sulfuric acid

_____

[2]

iii) the reaction between sodium hydrogen carbonate and nitric acid

_____

[2]

3 a) i) What is an acid anhydride?

_____

[1]

ii) Give TWO named examples of acid anhydrides.

1. _____

2. _____

[2]

A7 Acids, bases and salts (cont.)

b) i) What is ascorbic acid commonly known as?

_____

[1]

ii) Name the acid that builds up in muscles during strenuous exercise.

_____

[1]

iii) Sally was stung by an ant and two of her friends, Angela and Peter, gave suggestions as to how she should treat the sting.

Angela: I think you should treat it with vinegar.

Peter: I think you should treat it with sodium hydrogen carbonate.

Which of Sally's friends gave the correct advice? Why was this advice correct?

_____

_____

[2]

iv) Why can lime juice be used to remove rust stains?

_____

_____

[2]

4 a) i) State why ammonia is classified as an alkali.

_____

[1]

ii) Name TWO other alkalis.

1. _____

2. _____

[2]

b) Write a balanced chemical equation for EACH of the following base reactions.

i) calcium hydroxide reacting with ammonium chloride

_____

[2]

ii) the reaction between copper(II) oxide and ammonium sulfate

_____

[2]

iii) Emily noticed that when she added insoluble white lead(II) hydroxide to both nitric acid and sodium hydroxide solution, the lead(II) hydroxide disappeared and a colourless solution was left. Explain Emily's observations.

_____

_____

[2]

c) Draw a line to match EACH definition below with the type of oxide and give a named example of EACH type.

oxides of metals that react with acids	acidic oxides Example: _____
oxides of non-metals that don't react with acids or alkalis	basic oxides Example: _____
oxides of non-metals that react with alkalis	amphoteric oxides Example: _____
oxides of metals that react with both acids and strong alkalis	neutral oxides Example: _____

[8]

A7 Acids, bases and salts (cont.)

5 **a)** **i)** Define the term 'salt'.

_____

_____ [1]

ii) Distinguish between an acid salt and a normal salt.

_____

_____

_____ [2]

iii) Dibasic acids can form both acid salts and normal salts. What is a dibasic acid?

_____ [1]

iv) Write ONE balanced equation EACH for the formation of an acid salt and a normal salt when sulfuric acid reacts with aqueous sodium hydroxide:

- acid salt:

_____

- normal salt:

_____ [3]

b) **i)** Distinguish between a hydrated salt and an anhydrous salt.

_____

_____ [2]

ii) Give the formula of anhydrous copper(II) sulfate and hydrated copper(II) sulfate.

Anhydrous: _____

Hydrated: _____

[2]

c) i) Draw lines to match EACH of the following salts with its use.

an ingredient in baking powder	calcium sulphate
in the manufacture of cement	sodium hydrogen carbonate
in the manufacture of plaster of Paris	magnesium sulphate
to ease aches and pains and help cure skin problems	sodium nitrite
as a food preservative	calcium carbonate

[5]

ii) Give TWO possible dangers of using sodium nitrate to preserve food items.

1. _____

2. _____

[2]

6 a) i) Complete the table to give information about the solubility of EACH compound.

Compound	Solubility
sodium carbonate	
copper(II) nitrate	
lead(II) sulfate	
zinc hydroxide	
calcium chloride	
magnesium carbonate	
aluminium oxide	
potassium hydroxide	
ammonium chloride	
iron(II) sulfate	

[5]

A7 Acids, bases and salts (cont.)

b) The diagram below shows the steps Lynette used to prepare a pure sample of lead(II) chloride in the laboratory.

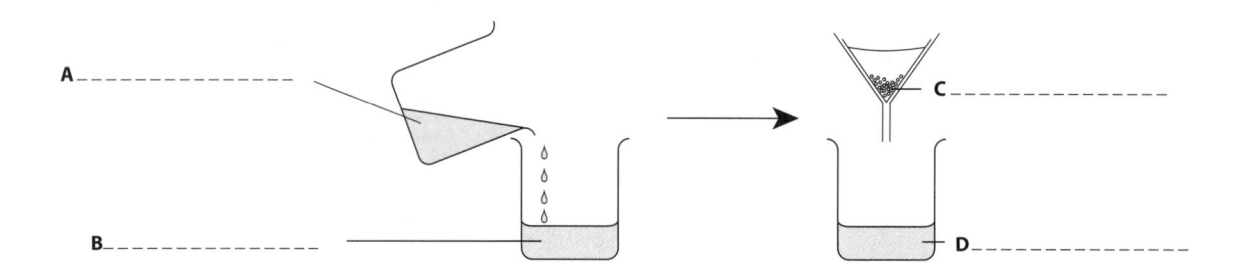

A ----------------

B ----------------

C ----------------

D ----------------

i) Label **A**, **B**, **C** and **D** on the lines provided. [4]

ii) Write an ionic equation for the reaction.

_____ [2]

iii) How did Lynette ensure that the sample of lead(II) chloride was pure?

_____ [1]

c) Simon wants to prepare a sample of copper(II) sulfate in the laboratory starting with copper(II) carbonate.

i) Name the other reactant he would use.

_____ [1]

ii) Write a balanced chemical equation for the reaction.

_____ [1]

iii) Simon adds the copper(II) carbonate to the other reactant until it is present in excess. Explain why he does this.

_____

_____

[1]

iv) What method would Simon use to obtain the copper(II) sulfate solution from the excess copper(II) carbonate?

_____

[1]

v) Simon then heats the solution to evaporate most of the water and leaves it to crystallise. Explain why he does this rather than evaporating all the water.

_____

_____

[2]

vi) Why would Simon not be able to make copper(II) sulfate by using copper in place of the copper(II) carbonate?

_____

[1]

d) Simon then decides to make a sample of sodium chloride.

i) What method would he use?

_____

[1]

ii) Why could Simon not make the sodium chloride by adding solid sodium carbonate to hydrochloric acid?

_____

_____

[2]

iii) Using the method named in **i)**, how would Simon be able to tell when the reaction had reached completion?

_____

_____

[2]

A7 Acids, bases and salts (cont.)

7 a) i) What is a neutralisation reaction?

_____

_____

[1]

ii) How does toothpaste help reduce tooth decay?

_____

_____

_____

[3]

iii) What is an antacid?

_____

_____

[2]

iv) Farmer Ted sometimes adds lime (calcium hydroxide) to his soil. Suggest why he does this.

_____

[1]

v) Farmer John advised Farmer Ted not to add an ammonium fertiliser at the same time as he added the lime. Suggest a reason for Farmer John's advice. Support your answer with a relevant equation.

Reason: _____

_____

_____

Equation: _____

[3]

b) To determine the mole ratio in which alkali **X** and acid **Y** react, Susan placed 25 cm³ of alkali **X** of concentration 1·0 mol dm⁻³ in a polystyrene cup and added acid **Y** of concentration 1·0 mol dm⁻³ from the burette. She stirred the solution and quickly recorded its temperature after each 2 cm³ of acid. The thermometer readings are shown below.

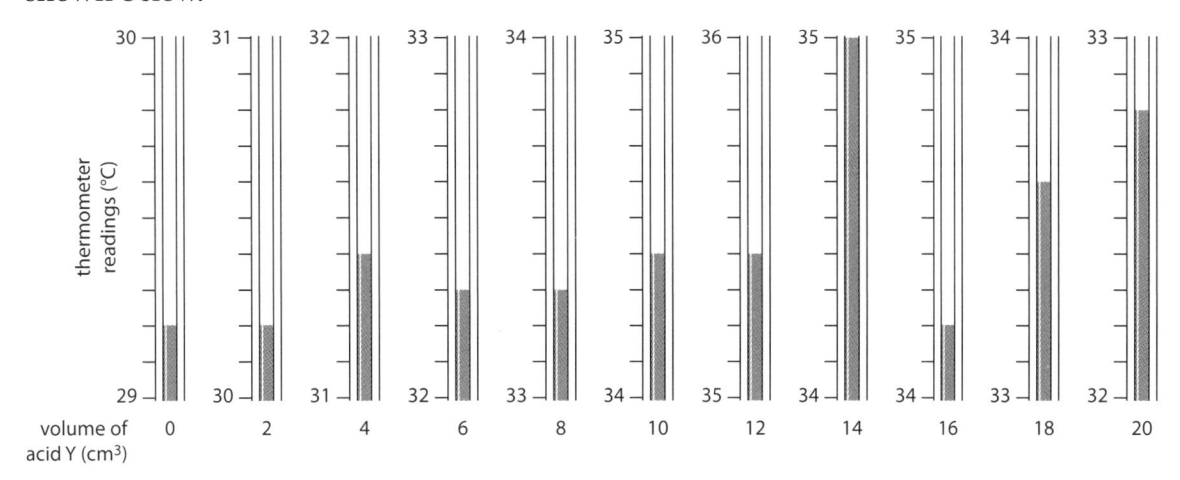

i) Why did Susan carry out the reaction in a polystyrene cup?

_____

_____

[2]

ii) Use the thermometer readings above to complete the table.

Volume of acid Y added (cm³)	Temperature of solution (°C)
0	29.5
2	30.5
4	31.5
6	32.5
8	33.5
10	34.5
12	35.5
14	35.0
16	34.5
18	34.0
20	33.0

[3]

A7 Acids, bases and salts (cont.)

iii) Plot temperature against volume of acid **Y** added and draw TWO straight lines of best fit.

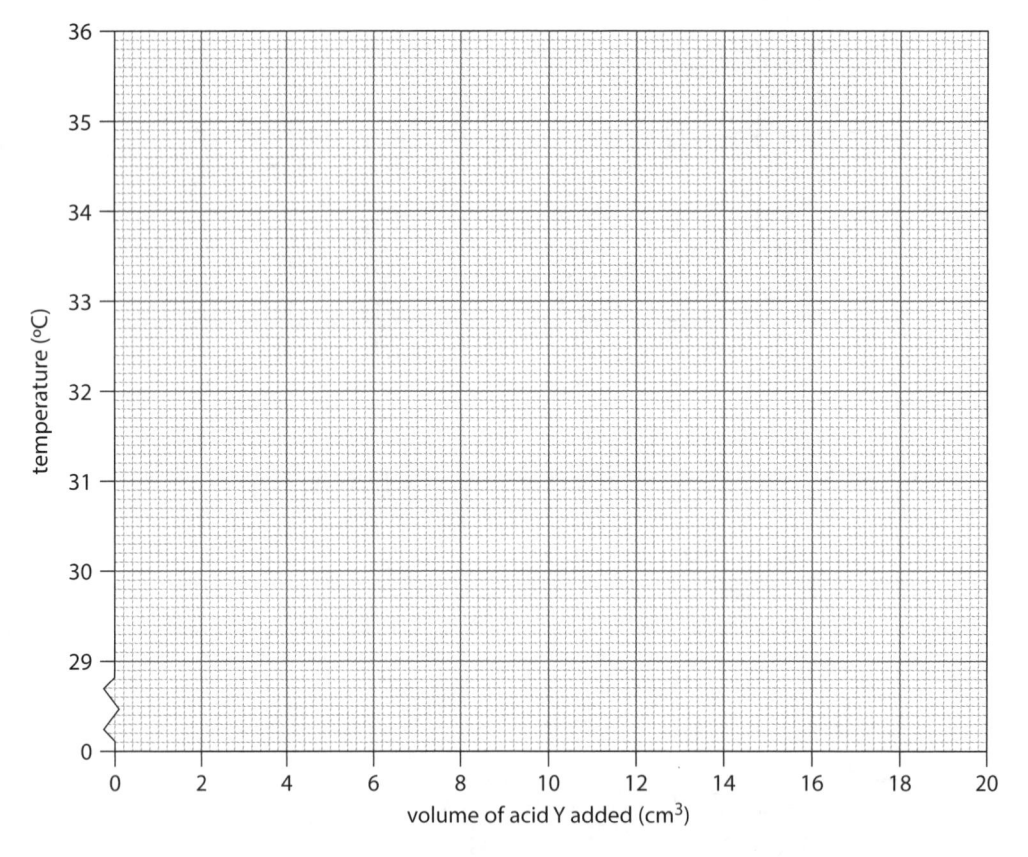

[3]

iv) Use your graph to determine the volume of acid **Y** needed to neutralise 25 cm³ of alkali **X**. _____ [1]

v) Determine the nearest whole number mole ratio in which alkali **X** and acid **Y** react.

[3]

8 To determine the concentration of a solution of sulfuric acid, Paul titrates the acid against 25·0 cm³ portions of sodium hydroxide solution of concentration 8·0 g dm⁻³, using a suitable indicator to identify the neutralisation point. Here are burette readings:

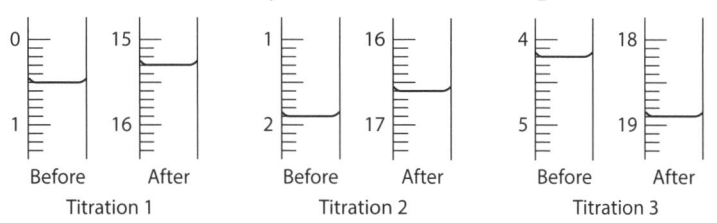

a) i) Name the piece of apparatus Paul would use to measure his 25·0 cm³ portions of sodium hydroxide solution.

_____

[1]

ii) What do you understand by the term 'neutralisation point'?

_____

_____

[1]

iii) Name a suitable indicator Paul could use to determine the neutralisation point.

_____

[1]

b) i) Use the burette readings above to complete the table below.

	Titration number		
	1	2	3
Final burette reading (cm³)			
Initial burette reading (cm³)			
Volume of acid added (cm³)			

[3]

ii) Determine the volume of sulfuric acid needed to neutralise 25 cm³ of sodium hydroxide solution.

[1]

A7 Acids, bases and salts (cont.)

iii) Calculate the number of moles of sodium hydroxide used in the titration.

[relative atomic masses: H = 1, Na = 23, O = 16]

[3]

iv) Write a balanced equation for the reaction.

_____

[2]

v) Determine the number of moles of sulfuric acid used in the titration.

[1]

vi) Determine the molar concentration of the sulfuric acid.

[1]

vii) Determine the mass concentration of the sulfuric acid.

[relative atomic masses: H = 1, O = 16, S = 32]

[2]

Total Marks .... / 137

A8 Oxidation–reduction reactions

1 **a)** Define EACH of the following in terms of electrons.

   i) oxidation: _____

   _____

   ii) reduction: _____

   _____
   [2]

b) Classify EACH of the following reactions as either oxidation or reduction. By reference to electrons, give a reason for your classification in EACH case.

   i) $Fe^{3+}(aq) + e^- \longrightarrow Fe^{2+}(aq)$

   Type of reaction: _____ Reason: _____

   _____
   [2]

   ii) $Al(s) \longrightarrow Al^{3+}(aq) + 3e^-$

   Type of reaction: _____ Reason: _____

   _____
   [2]

   iii) The formation of the oxide ion (O^{2-}) when oxygen reacts with calcium.

   Ionic half equation for the reaction:

   _____
   [2]

   Type of reaction: _____ Reason: _____

   _____
   [2]

c) Define EACH of the following in terms of oxidation number.

   i) oxidation: _____

   _____
   [1]

A8 Oxidation–reduction reactions (cont.)

ii) reduction: _____

_____

[1]

d) i) Determine the oxidation number of sulfur in sulfur trioxide (SO$_3$) and give an alternative name for sulfur trioxide.

Alternative name: _____

[2]

ii) Determine the oxidation number of nitrogen in the nitrite ion (NO$_2^-$) and give an alternative name for the ion.

Alternative name: _____

[2]

iii) Determine the oxidation number of chlorine in the ClO$_4^-$ ion and name the ion.

Name: _____

[2]

iv) Determine the change in oxidation number of nitrogen in the following reaction and use this to decide if the ammonia has been oxidised or reduced.

$$2NH_3(g) + 3CuO(s) \longrightarrow N_2(g) + 3Cu(s) + 3H_2O(l)$$

_____

[3]

e) State, with reasons based on oxidation number, which reactant has been oxidised and which has been reduced in EACH of the following reactions.

   i) Mg(s) + CuSO$_4$(aq) ⟶ MgSO$_4$(aq) + Cu(s)

   _____

   _____

   _____
   [2]

   ii) Fe$_2$O$_3$(s) + 3CO(g) ⟶ 2Fe(s) + 3CO$_2$(g)

   _____

   _____

   _____
   [2]

2 a) In terms of oxidation number, what is EACH of the following?

   i) an oxidising agent: _____

   _____
   [1]

   ii) a reducing agent: _____

   _____
   [1]

b) State, with a reason based on oxidation number, if sulfur is acting as an oxidising agent or a reducing agent in each of the following reactions.

   i) S(s) + O$_2$(g) ⟶ SO$_2$(g)

   _____

   _____
   [2]

   ii) Mg(s) + S(s) ⟶ MgS(s)

   _____

   _____
   [2]

A8 Oxidation–reduction reactions (cont.)

c) Using oxidation number to support your answer, state which reactant is acting as an oxidising agent and which is acting as a reducing agent in the following reaction.

$$CH_4(g) + 4CuO(s) \longrightarrow 4Cu(s) + CO_2(g) + 2H_2O(g)$$

_____

_____

_____

_____

[2]

d) i) Three chemistry students find a bottle of a colourless liquid in the laboratory and each makes a different suggestion about the identity of its contents.

Josh: I think it is an oxidising agent.

Richard: I think that it is neither an oxidising nor a reducing agent.

Matthieu: I think it is a reducing agent.

Complete the following table to summarise TWO different tests the students could use to find out whose suggestion is correct.

Test reagent	Results of test if:		
	Josh's suggestion is correct	Richard's suggestion is correct	Matthieu's suggestion is correct

[6]

52

ii) Assuming Matthieu's suggestion is correct, explain the reason for the colour change he observed and suggest a second reagent he could use to confirm that he is correct.

Explanation: _____

_____

Reagent: _____

_____

[2]

iii) Name one substance that behaves as both an oxidising agent and a reducing agent.

_____

[1]

e) By referring to oxidation and reduction, explain EACH of the following statements.

i) The cut surface of an apple turns brown if the apple is left uneaten on a plate.

_____

_____

[1]

ii) Sodium chlorate(I) is a good bleaching agent.

_____

_____

[1]

iii) Sodium sulfite is a good preservative of some food items.

_____

_____

[2]

iv) Iron nails rust very easily when exposed to moist air.

_____

_____

[1]

Total Marks _____ / 47

A9 Electrochemistry

1 a) i) Distinguish between a conductor and a non-conductor.

_____

_____

[1]

ii) Draw lines to classify EACH of the following substances as a conductor or a non-conductor.

- graphite
- solid sodium chloride
- copper(II) sulfate solution
- aqueous nitric acid
- carbon tetrachloride
- sulfur

conductor

non-conductor

[3]

b) i) What is an electrolyte?

_____

_____

[1]

ii) Distinguish between a strong and a weak electrolyte.

_____

_____

_____

[2]

iii) Why is pure water classified as a weak electrolyte?

_____

_____

[2]

iv) Complete the table below to give TWO differences between metallic conduction and electrolytic conduction.

Metallic conduction	Electrolytic conduction

[4]

c) i) Define EACH of the following terms.

electrolysis: _____

_____

anode: _____

_____

cathode: _____

_____

[3]

ii) Why does oxidation occur at the anode and reduction occur at the cathode during electrolysis?

_____

_____

[2]

d) The diagram below shows the electrolysis of molten lead(II) bromide using inert graphite electrodes.

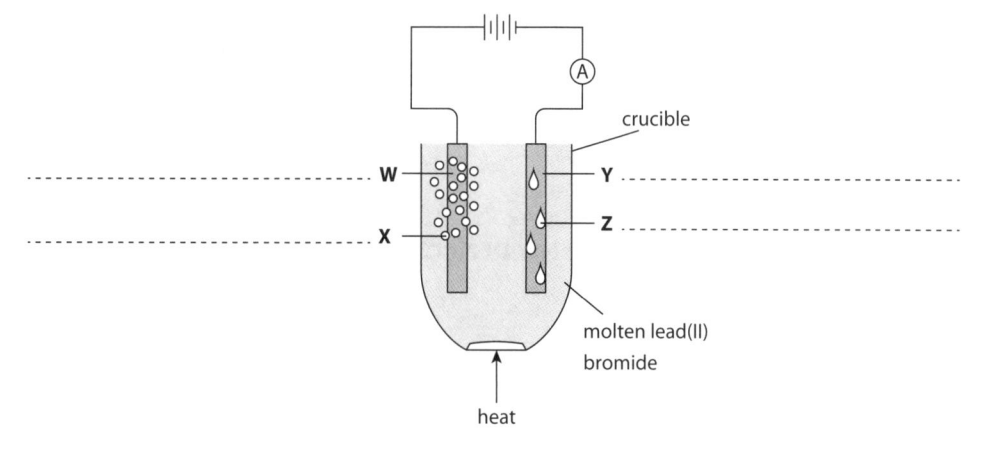

i) Label **W, X, Y** and **Z** on the lines provided on the diagram above.

[4]

55

A9 Electrochemistry (cont.)

ii) Write ionic equations to show the formation of **X** and **Z**.

X: _____

Z: _____

[4]

2 The electrochemical series of metals can be used to predict various chemical reactions.

a) What is the electrochemical series of metals?

_____

[1]

b) Metal **F** is above zinc in the electrochemical series. Would you expect **F** to react with zinc sulfate solution? Give a reason for your answer.

_____

_____

[2]

c) Metal **G** is below hydrogen in the electrochemical series. Would you expect **G** to react with hydrochloric acid? Give a reason for your answer.

_____

_____

[2]

d) Write an equation for the reaction between magnesium and copper(II) sulfate solution.

_____

[1]

3 a) List the THREE factors that affect the preferential discharge of anions during the electrolysis of aqueous solutions.

1. _____

2. _____

3. _____

[3]

b) Rachel set up two electrolytic cells to electrolyse sodium chloride solution. Cell **A** contained a very dilute solution and cell **B** contained a concentrated solution. What difference, if any, would there be in:

  i) the reaction occurring at the anode in EACH cell?

  _____

  _____

  _____
  [2]

  ii) the reaction occurring at the cathode in EACH cell?

  _____

  _____
  [1]

  iii) the events occurring in the electrolyte of EACH cell?

  _____

  _____
  [2]

c) Sabrina decided to electrolyse dilute sulfuric acid in the laboratory using the following apparatus.

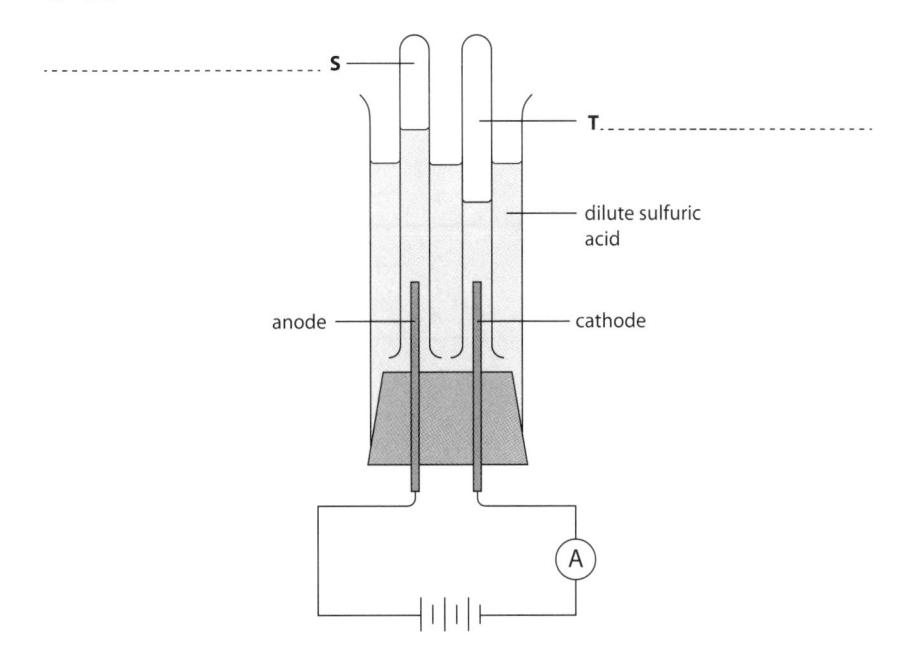

  i) Identify **S** and **T** on the lines provided on the diagram above. [2]

A9 Electrochemistry (cont.)

ii) Write relevant equations to show the formation of **S** and **T**.

S: _____

T: _____

[4]

iii) Account for the different volumes of **S** and **T** indicated in the diagram.

_____

_____

[2]

d) Amy set up an electrolytic cell to electrolyse a solution of copper(II) sulfate using graphite electrodes. Describe, giving a reason in EACH case, what she observed:

i) at the anode:

Observation: _____

Reason: _____

_____

[2]

ii) at the cathode (your reason should include a relevant equation):

Observation: _____

Reason: _____

_____

_____

[4]

iii) in the electrolyte:

Observation: _____

Reason: _____

[2]

iv) Amy then replaced the graphite electrodes with ones made of copper. Describe, giving a reason and relevant equation, what she observed at the anode.

Observation: _____

Reason: _____

_____

_____

[4]

4 a) i) Define the Faraday constant.

_____

[1]

ii) What determines the quantity of substances produced at the electrodes during electrolysis?

_____

[1]

b) A steady current of 2·5 A flows for 2 hours, 8 minutes and 40 seconds through dilute sodium chloride solution.

i) Calculate the quantity of electricity flowing.

[1]

ii) Write an equation for the reaction occurring at the anode.

_____

[1]

iii) Determine the number of moles of oxygen produced at the anode.

[2]

A9 Electrochemistry (cont.)

c) How long must a steady current of 5·0 A flow through dilute sulfuric acid to produce 3·0 g of hydrogen at the cathode?
[relative atomic mass: H = 1]

[4]

5 a) i) What is the process of anodising used for?

_____

_____
[1]

ii) Suggest TWO reasons for anodising a saucepan.

1. _____

2. _____
[2]

b) i) James wishes to demonstrate the principles of electroplating a spoon with silver to his fellow students. What would he use as the anode, the cathode and the electrolyte?

the anode _____

the cathode _____

the electrolyte _____
[3]

ii) Write ionic equations for the reaction occurring at EACH electrode during the electroplating process:

at the anode _____

at the cathode _____

[2]

iii) Calculate the increase in mass of the spoon if James allows a current of 2·0 A to flow for 32 minutes and 10 seconds through the electrode.

[3]

c) i) Electrolysis can be used to purify metals. Briefly outline the method used to purify a lump of copper.

_____

_____

_____

_____

[4]

ii) Explain why electrolysis is not suitable for purifying metals above hydrogen in the electrochemical series.

_____

_____

[2]

Total Marks _____ / 89

61

A10 Rates of reaction

1 **a)** Define 'rate of reaction'.

_____

_____

[1]

b) To determine how the rate of a reaction varies as the reaction proceeds, Keenan reacted calcium carbonate crystals with excess hydrochloric acid and measured the volume of carbon dioxide produced every 30 seconds. His results are in the table below.

Time/s	Volume of carbon dioxide/cm^3
0	0
30	54
60	88
90	106
120	118
150	126
180	128
210	128
240	128

i) In the space provided draw a labelled diagram to show how Keenan would have set up the apparatus to conduct his experiment.

[3]

ii) Plot Keenan's results on the graph paper below.

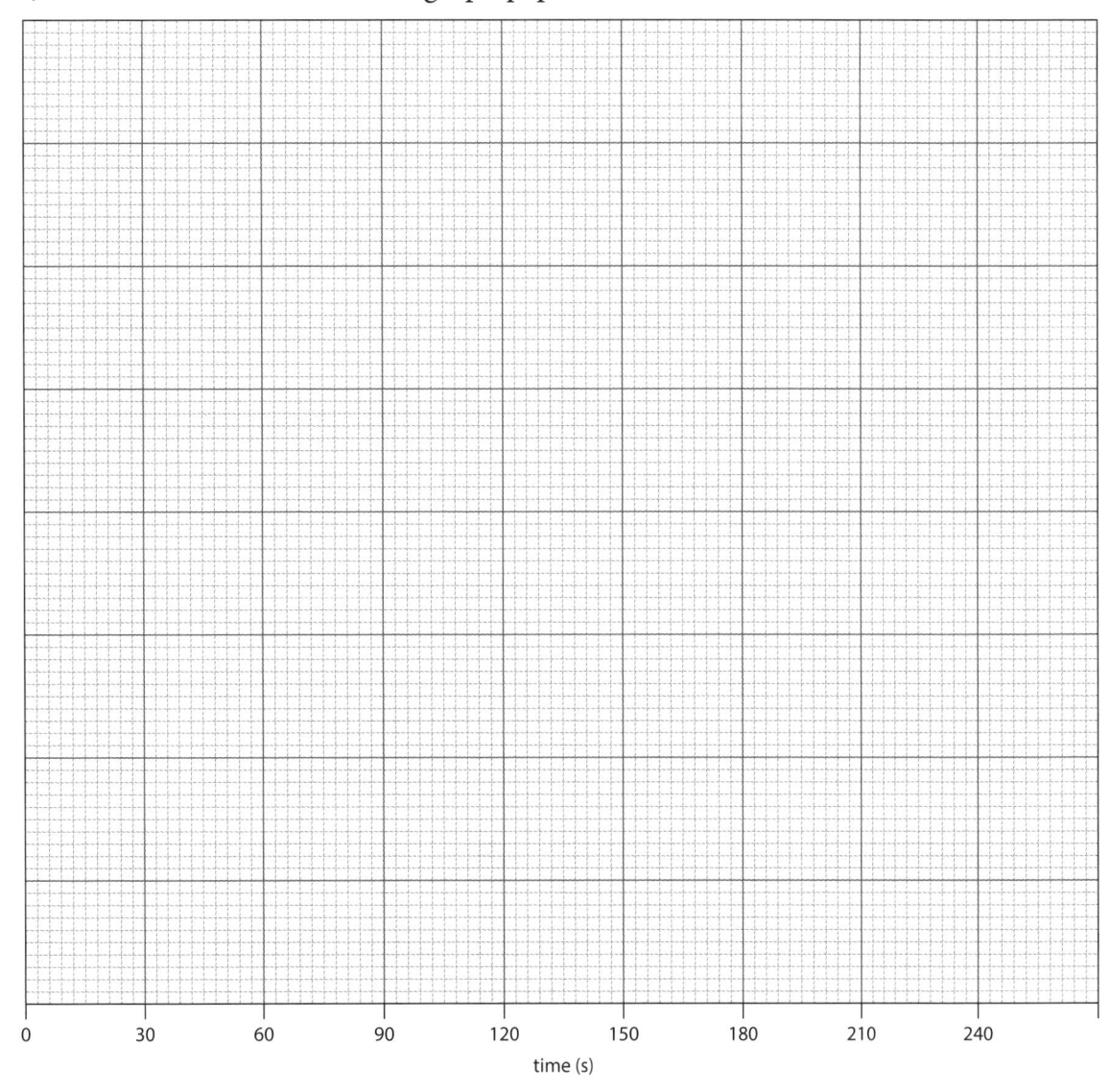

[3]

iii) Use the results to determine the average rate of the reaction in $cm^3 \ s^{-1}$:

in the first minute:

[1]

in the second minute:

[1]

A10 Rates of reaction (cont.)

iv) By reference to the collision theory for a reaction, explain why the average rate of the reaction was higher in the first minute than in the second minute.

_____

_____

_____
[3]

v) Explain what happened after 180 s.

_____

_____
[1]

2 a) List FOUR factors that affect the rate of a reaction.

1. _____ 2. _____

3. _____ 4. _____
[4]

b) To investigate the effect of changing various factors on the rate of a reaction, Kayla placed a conical flask onto a balance at room temperature and added 5·0 g of magnesium ribbon followed by excess hydrochloric acid of concentration 0·5 mol dm^{-3}. She weighed the flask and its contents at regular intervals and plotted her results as shown:

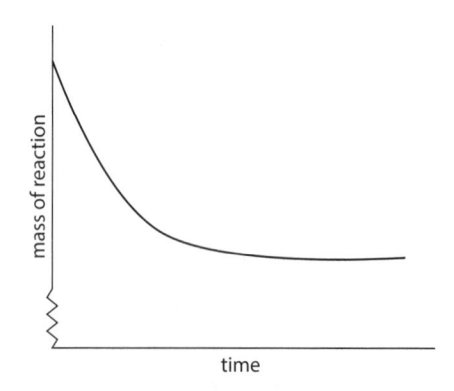

i) Kayla repeated her experiment using 5·0 g of magnesium powder in place of the ribbon. Draw a second curve on the figure above to show the results of her second experiment. [2]

ii) By referring to the collision theory for reactions, explain the gradient of the curve you drew in **i)**.

_____

_____

[2]

iii) Kayla repeated her experiment again at 40°C. What effect would you expect this to have had on the rate of the reaction? Explain your answer.

Effect: _____

Explanation: _____

_____

_____

_____

[4]

iv) Kayla repeated her experiment again using excess hydrochloric acid of concentration 0.25 mol dm^{-3}. What effect would you expect this to have had on the rate of the reaction? Explain your answer.

Effect: _____

Explanation: _____

_____

_____

[3]

c) i) What is a catalyst?

_____

[1]

ii) How does a catalyst work to speed up a chemical reaction?

_____

_____

_____

[2]

Total Marks _____ / 31

A11 Energetics

1 **a)** Distinguish between an exothermic reaction and an endothermic reaction.

_____

_____

_____

[2]

b) The diagram below shows the energy profile diagram for a reaction.

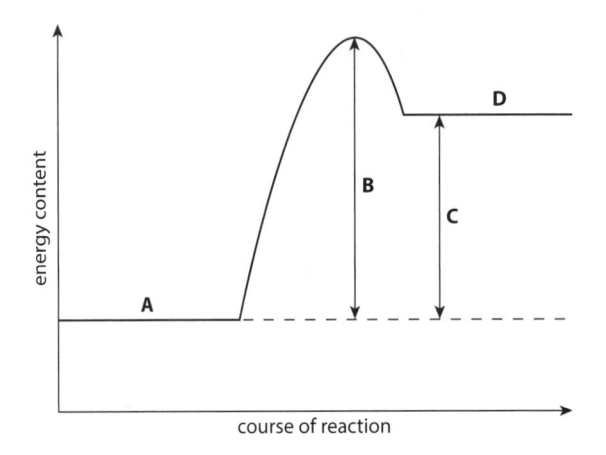

i) State, with a reason, whether the reaction is exothermic or endothermic.

_____

_____

_____

[2]

ii) Identify **A**, **B**, **C** and **D**.

A: _____ B: _____

C: _____ D: _____

[4]

iii) On the diagram above, show the effect of adding a catalyst to the reaction. [1]

iv) Would ΔH be positive or negative?

_____

[1]

c) The reaction between zinc and sulfuric acid is shown in the following equation.

$$Zn(s) + H_2SO_4(aq) \longrightarrow ZnSO_4(aq) + H_2(g) \quad \Delta H \text{ −ve}$$

i) Is the reaction exothermic or endothermic?

_____

[1]

ii) How did you deduce your answer to **i)** above?

_____

[1]

iii) Explain the enthalpy change that occurs during the reaction.

_____

_____

[2]

2 a) i) Define 'heat of neutralisation'.

_____

_____

[1]

ii) Explain why the heats of neutralisation for the reaction between potassium hydroxide and nitric acid, and for the reaction between sodium hydroxide and sulfuric acid, have the same value.

_____

_____

_____

[2]

b) To determine the heat of neutralisation, Chelsea placed 50 cm³ of sodium hydroxide solution of concentration 1.0 mol dm⁻³ in a polystyrene cup and recorded its temperature. She then recorded the temperature of 50 cm³ of sulfuric acid, added it to the cup, stirred the solution and recorded its maximum temperature, as follows:

- initial temperature of NaOH(aq) = 29·5 °C
- initial temperature of H_2SO_4(aq) = 29·9 °C
- maximum temperature of the solution = 35·8 °C

A11 Energetics (cont.)

i) Calculate the increase in temperature.

[2]

ii) Determine the heat change for the reaction assuming that the specific heat capacity of the solution is $4.2 \text{ J g}^{-1} \text{ °C}^{-1}$.

[1]

iii) State TWO other assumptions you made in calculating **ii)** above.

1. _____

2. _____

[2]

iv) Write a balanced equation for the reaction.

_____

[2]

v) Given that the sodium hydroxide is the limiting reactant, determine the number of moles of water made in the reaction.

[2]

vi) Calculate the heat of neutralisation.

[1]

vii) Draw a fully labelled energy profile diagram for the reaction.

[3]

c) Define 'heat of solution'.

[1]

d) Ashlee dissolved 6·06 g of potassium nitrate in 75 cm³ of water in an insulated container and recorded a temperature decrease of 5·7 °C.

   i) Calculate the heat of solution of potassium nitrate, assuming that the specific heat capacity of the solution is 4·2 J g⁻¹ °C⁻¹.

[3]

   ii) Is the reaction exothermic or endothermic? _____ [1]

   iii) By referring to bonds breaking and bonds forming, explain the energy change that occurred.

[3]

Total Marks _____ / 38

B1 Sources of hydrocarbon compounds

1 a) i) What are hydrocarbons?

_____

[1]

ii) Natural gas and petroleum (crude oil) are two natural sources of hydrocarbons. Name the FOUR gases that make up natural gas.

1. _____   2. _____

3. _____   4. _____

[2]

iii) What is petroleum?

_____

_____

[2]

iv) Name the process by which petroleum is separated into different components.

_____

[1]

v) Complete the following sentence.

Crude oil is separated into different fractions in a _____ _____

[1]

vi) Outline the principles involved in the separation process you named in **iv)** above.

_____

_____

_____

_____

_____

[4]

b) Complete the table below so it provides information about any FOUR fractions obtained during the process named in **iv)** on the previous page TWO uses of EACH fraction named.

Name of fraction	Use 1	Use 2

[8]

2 a) When crude oil is separated into different components, many of these are 'cracked'.

   i) What occurs during cracking?

   _____

   _____

   [1]

   ii) Cracking can be carried out in TWO ways. Name these and distinguish between them both.

   1. _____

   _____

   2. _____

   _____

   [4]

   iii) Explain TWO reasons why cracking is important in the petroleum industry.

   1. _____

   _____

   _____

   [2]

B1 Sources of hydrocarbon compounds (cont.)

2. _____

_____

_____

[2]

b) Show, using fully displayed structural formulae, THREE ways in which pentane (C_5H_{12}) can be cracked. In EACH case name the products of the cracking process below their structures.

[9]

Total Marks _____ / 37

B2 Organic chemistry – an introduction

1 a) i) Draw a dot-and-cross diagram to show bonding in the methane (CH_4) molecule.
(atomic numbers: C = 6, H = 1)

[2]

ii) Why is carbon able to form a huge number of different organic compounds?

_____

_____

[1]

iii) Support your answer to **ii)** above by using diagrams to show how:

- four carbon atoms bond with single bonds to form a straight chain molecule with the formula C_4H_{10}
- two carbon atoms bond with a double bond to form a compound with the formula C_2H_4
- five carbon atoms bond with single bonds to form a branched chain molecule with the formula C_5H_{12}

C_4H_{10} $\qquad\qquad\qquad$ C_2H_4 $\qquad\qquad\qquad$ C_5H_{12}

[3]

B2 Organic chemistry – an introduction (cont.)

b) i) What is a homologous series?

_____

[1]

ii) Give FOUR characteristics of a homologous series.

1. _____

2. _____

3. _____

4. _____

[4]

c) The fully displayed formulae of four different organic compounds are given below.

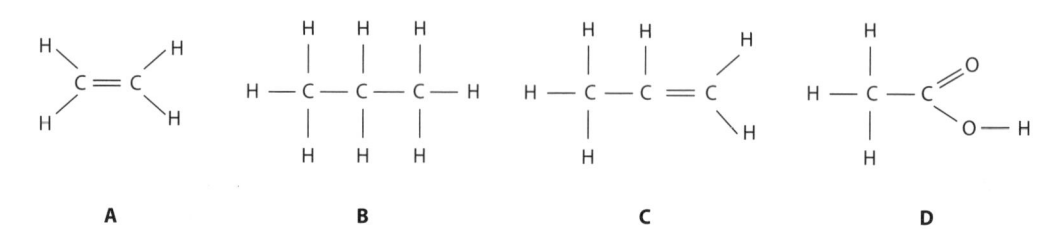

A   B   C   D

i) Which TWO compounds belong to the same homologous series?

_____

[1]

ii) To which homologous series do the compounds named in i) belong?

_____

[1]

iii) Give a reason for your answer to ii).

_____

[1]

iv) Give the general formula for the series named in ii).

_____

[1]

d) Complete the following table.

Name of compound	Name of homologous series	Condensed formula of compound	Fully displayed structural formula of compound
ethane			
butene			
propanoic acid			
methanol			

[6]

e) Name EACH of the following compounds.

i) C_3H_7COOH _____ ii) C_4H_8 _____

iii) C_5H_{12} _____ iv) CH_3CH_2OH _____

[4]

2 a) i) Define the term 'structural isomerism'.

_____

_____

[1]

ii) In what TWO ways is it possible to form structural isomers of straight chain molecules?

1. _____

2. _____

[2]

B2 Organic chemistry – an introduction (cont.)

b) Name the following structural isomers of pentane.

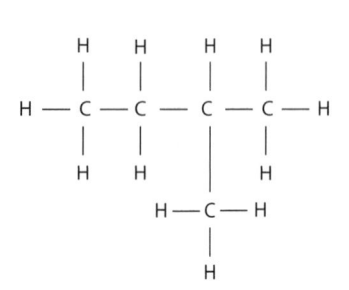

_____   _____ [2]

c) i) Hexane (C_6H_{14}) has five structural isomers. Draw and name any TWO of these.

_____   _____ [4]

ii) Pentene (C_5H_{10}) has TWO unbranched isomers. Draw and name these.

_____   _____ [4]

Total Marks _____ / 42

B3 Reactions of carbon compounds

1 a) i) Alkanes are referred to as being 'saturated'. What does this mean?

_____

[1]

   ii) How does the fact that alkanes are saturated affect their reactivity?

_____

_____

[2]

b) Alkanes burn very easily in air.

   i) Write a balanced chemical equation for EACH of the following reactions.

   Methane burning in air _____

   Propane burning in air _____

[2]

   ii) Are the reactions exothermic or endothermic? Explain how you arrived at your answer.

_____

_____

[2]

   iii) Describe what the flame would look like when methane is burning in a plentiful air supply.

_____

[1]

   iv) Explain why the flame has the appearance described in **iii)**.

_____

_____

[2]

77

B3 Reactions of carbon compounds (cont.)

c) Given the right condition, methane will react with chlorine gas.

   i) What condition is required for the reaction? _____

   [1]

   ii) Name the type of reaction occurring and explain what happens during the reaction.

   Type of reaction: _____ Explanation: _____

   _____

   [2]

   iii) Write a chemical equation to show the first stage in the reaction and name the products.

   Equation: _____

   Names of products: _____

   [2]

   iv) Write a balanced chemical equation for the overall reaction occurring between methane and chlorine, and name the final organic product.

   Equation: _____

   Name of organic product: _____

   [3]

d) i) Give THREE reasons why alkanes are used so extensively as fuels.

   1. _____

   2. _____

   3. _____

   [3]

   ii) Why are alkanes used as solvents?

   _____

   _____

   [1]

iii) What is biogas and how is it produced?

_____

_____

[2]

iv) Give TWO points you could make to support the statement that 'the production of biogas is beneficial to the environment'.

1. _____

2. _____

[2]

2 a) i) Alkenes are described as being 'unsaturated'. What do you understand by this?

_____

[1]

ii) How does the fact that alkenes are unsaturated affect their reactivity? Explain your answer.

_____

_____

_____

_____

[3]

b) Under the right conditions, ethene reacts with water.

i) State the conditions required for ethene to react with water.

_____

_____

_____

_____

[4]

ii) Name the type of reaction occurring.

_____

[1]

B3 Reactions of carbon compounds (cont.)

iii) Complete the following equation to show the structure of the product.

$$\begin{array}{c}H\\H\end{array}C=C\begin{array}{c}H\\H\end{array} + H_2O \longrightarrow$$

iv) Name the compound formed in the reaction. _____

[1]

c) The diagram below shows the structural formula of one member of the alkene series.

$$H-\underset{H}{\overset{H}{C}}-\underset{H}{\overset{H}{C}}-\overset{H}{C}=\overset{H}{C}-\underset{H}{\overset{H}{C}}-H$$

i) What might you observe when this compound reacts with bromine solution?

_____

[1]

ii) Draw the structural formula of the compound formed during the reaction referred to in **i)** and name the compound formed.

_____

[2]

d) Propene reacts with hydrogen if the conditions are right.

i) State the conditions required and write an equation for the reaction.

Conditions: _____

Equation: _____

[3]

ii) Name the product of the reaction. _____

[1]

e) Jason finds two bottles containing colourless liquids in a cupboard in the laboratory and two labels, which appear to have dropped off the bottles, are at the back of the cupboard. The labels are shown below.

CYCLOHEXENE   CYCLOHEXANE

i) Jason wants to replace the labels on the correct bottles. Name one reagent, other than bromine solution, that he could use.

_____

[1]

ii) State the results he would expect when he tests EACH liquid and explain how his results would enable him to relabel the bottles correctly.

_____

_____

_____

_____

[4]

3 a) Below are FOUR organic compounds, **A, B, C** and **D**.

A   B   C   D

i) Which compounds belong to the same homologous series?

_____

[1]

ii) Name the homologous series and state why you placed the compounds named in **i)** in this series.

Series: _____ Reason: _____

_____

[2]

iii) What type of compound is **C**?

_____

[1]

B3 Reactions of carbon compounds (cont.)

iv) Would you expect compound **D** to be soluble or insoluble in water? Give a reason for your answer.

_____

_____

[3]

v) Draw and name fully displayed formulae of TWO straight chain isomers of **B**.

_____   _____

[4]

b) The reaction scheme below summarises some of the reactions of ethanol (**Q**). Study the reaction scheme and answer the questions that follow.

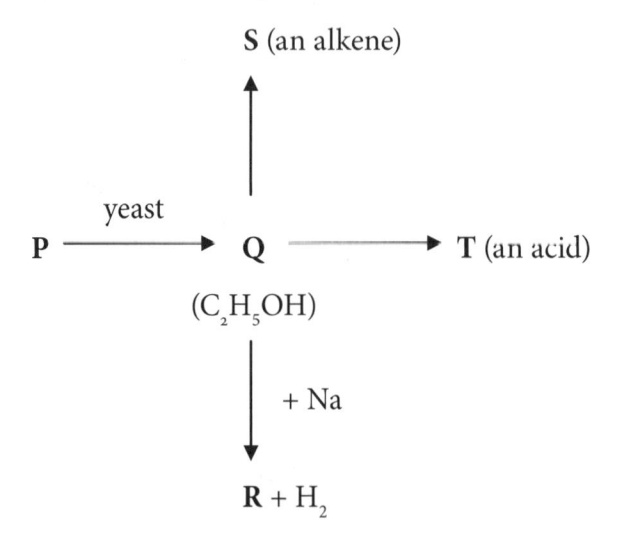

$$P \xrightarrow{\text{yeast}} Q \longrightarrow T \text{ (an acid)}$$

with **S** (an alkene) above **Q**, and **Q** (C_2H_5OH) reacting with $+ Na$ downward to give **R** + H_2.

i) The name and molecular formula of **P** is: _____

The type of reaction in converting **P** to **Q** is: _____

[3]

ii) By what process would you obtain a pure sample of **Q** from the reaction mixture?

_____

[1]

iii) Write an equation for the reaction between **Q** and sodium, and identify **R**.

Equation: _____

Identity of **R**: _____

[3]

iv) Give the reaction conditions for the conversion of **Q** to **S** and write an equation for the reaction.

Conditions: _____

Equation: _____

[3]

v) Name the type of reaction involved in the conversion of **Q** to **S**.

_____

[1]

vi) Identify compound **T** and draw its fully displayed structural formula.

Identity of **T**: _____

Structural formula of **T**:

[2]

vii) Name the reagent needed to convert **Q** to **T** in the laboratory and identify the type of reaction involved.

Reagent: _____

Type of reaction: _____

[2]

c) i) What is the breathalyser test used for?

_____

[1]

B3 Reactions of carbon compounds (cont.)

ii) Explain the chemical principles of the breathalyser test.

_____

_____

_____
[3]

4 a) i) Give the general formula for an alkanoic acid. _____
[1]

ii) Give the condensed formula for EACH of the following alkanoic acids.

propanoic acid: _____   methanoic acid: _____
[2]

iii) Using ethanoic acid as an example, explain why aqueous solutions of alkanoic acids react in a similar way to inorganic acids such as hydrochloric acid. Support your answer with a relevant equation.

Explanation: _____

_____

Equation: _____
[3]

iv) What difference would you expect to observe between the reaction of an alkanoic acid with a metal and that of an inorganic acid with a metal? Give a reason for the difference.

Difference: _____

Reason: _____

_____

_____
[3]

v) Write a balanced chemical equation for EACH of the following reactions:

the reaction between ethanoic acid and sodium hydroxide

_____

the reaction between ethanoic acid and calcium carbonate

_____

[3]

b) The reaction scheme below summarises some other reactions of ethanoic acid (**X**). Study the reaction scheme and answer the questions that follow.

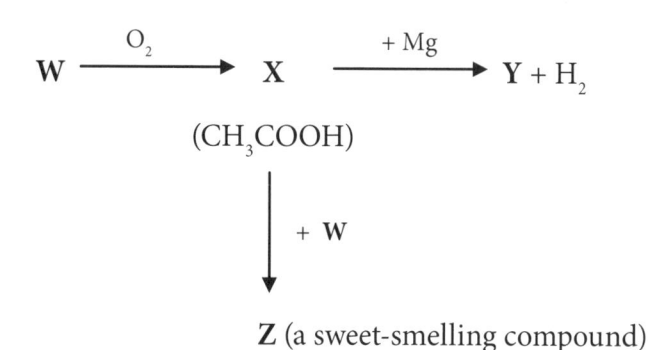

$$W \xrightarrow{O_2} X \xrightarrow{+ Mg} Y + H_2$$
$$(CH_3COOH)$$
$$\downarrow + W$$
$$Z \text{ (a sweet-smelling compound)}$$

i) Identify **W**. _____

[1]

ii) Name the type of reaction by which **W** is converted to **X**.

_____

[1]

iii) Write an equation for the reaction between **X** and **W**, and identify **Z**.

Equation: _____

Identity of **Z**: _____

[2]

iv) Name the type of reaction by which **W** and **X** are converted to **Z**.

_____

[1]

v) Write an equation for the reaction between **X** and magnesium, and identify **Y**.

Equation: _____

Identity of **Y**: _____

[2]

5 a) i) What are esters?

_____

[1]

B3 Reactions of carbon compounds (cont.)

ii) To make a sample of ethyl ethanoate in the laboratory, Kaylie heated 10 cm³ of ethanoic acid with 10 cm³ of ethanol and 2 cm³ of concentrated sulfuric acid under reflux. Give TWO reasons why she added the concentrated sulfuric acid.

Reason 1: _____

_____

Reason 2: _____

_____
[2]

b) i) Name EACH of the following FOUR esters.

$C_3H_7COOC_2H_5$ _____ $HCOOC_4H_9$ _____

H H O   H
| | ‖ |
H—C—C—C—O—C—H
| | |
H H   H

H O   H H H
| ‖ | | |
H—C—C—O—C—C—C—H
| | | |
H   H H H

_____   _____
[4]

ii) Write the condensed formulae for these substances:

methyl butanoate _____

butyl ethanoate _____
[2]

iii) Draw the fully displayed structural formulae of the following esters.

ethyl methanoate   propyl propanoate
[2]

c) Esters can be hydrolysed in two different ways.

   i) What occurs when esters are hydrolysed?

   _____

   [1]

   ii) Write a balanced equation to show what happens when ethyl ethanoate is hydrolysed by being boiled with sodium hydroxide solution.

   _____

   [1]

   iii) The following ester was hydrolysed by being boiled with dilute hydrochloric acid.

   $$CH_3CH_2\overset{\displaystyle O}{\overset{\|}{C}}OCH_3$$

   Name the products formed and give the formula of EACH.

   Product 1: _____

   Product 2: _____

   [4]

d) The ester glyceryl octadecanoate (($C_{17}H_{35}COO)_3C_3H_5$) can be hydrolysed by boiling with concentrated sodium hydroxide solution.

   i) Name the type of reaction occurring. _____

   [1]

   ii) Write a balanced chemical equation for the reaction.

   _____

   [2]

   iii) Name the products of the reaction.

   _____

   [2]

e) i) What is a detergent?

   _____

   [1]

B3 Reactions of carbon compounds (cont.)

ii) Distinguish between soapy and soapless detergents.

_____

_____

[2]

iii) Give ONE advantage and TWO disadvantages of using a soapless detergent compared with using a soapy detergent.

Advantage: _____

_____

Disadvantages: _____

_____

_____

_____

[3]

6 a) Define the term 'polymer'.

_____

_____

[1]

b) Polymers are formed by polymerisation. Complete the following table to give THREE differences between addition polymerisation and condensation polymerisation.

Addition polymerisation	Condensation polymerisation

[6]

c) The structures of three monomers, **Q**, **R** and **S**, are given below.

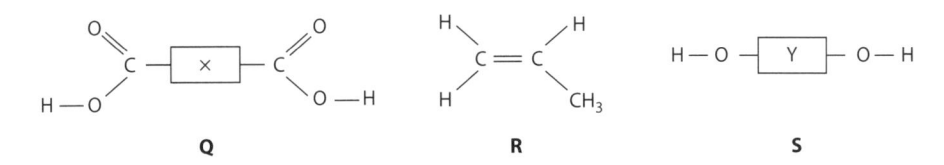

[Structures shown: **Q** is HO–OC–[X]–CO–OH (dicarboxylic acid); **R** is CH₂=CH(CH₃) (propene); **S** is H–O–[Y]–O–H (diol)]

i) Using TWO molecules of **Q** and TWO molecules of **S**, show the partial structure of the polymer they form when they are linked together.

[2]

ii) Identify the type of polymerisation reaction occurring and name the type of polymer drawn in **i)** above:

Type of polymerisation: _____

Type of polymer: _____
[2]

iii) Give a named example of the polymer drawn in **i)**.

_____
[1]

iv) What is the name given to the linkages between the monomer units?

_____
[1]

v) Draw the partial structure of the polymer formed when three molecules of **R** polymerise.

[1]

89

B3 Reactions of carbon compounds (cont.)

vi) • What is the type of polymerisation occurring in **v)**? _____

• What is the type of polymer drawn in **v)**? _____

[2]

d) The partial structure of a protein molecule is shown below.

$$-N-\boxed{}-\overset{\overset{O}{\|}}{C}-N-\boxed{}-\overset{\overset{O}{\|}}{C}-N-\boxed{}-\overset{\overset{O}{\|}}{C}-$$
$$\;\;\;|\qquad\qquad\quad\;\;|\qquad\qquad\quad\;\;|$$
$$\;\;\;H\qquad\qquad\quad H\qquad\qquad\quad H$$

i) Name the type of polymer shown. _____

[1]

ii) Draw the structure of the monomer unit of the polymer shown above.

[2]

e) Draw lines to match EACH of the following polymers with its use.

nylon	to make pipe fittings
polychloroethene (polyvinylchloride–PVC)	to make plastic bottles for soft drinks
polystyrene	to make fishing lines
polyethylene terephthalate (PET)	stored as a food reserve in living organisms
starch	to make fast-food containers

[5]

Total Marks _____ / 148

C1 Characteristics of metals

1 a) i) In terms of atomic structure, what is a metal?

_____

_____
[1]

ii) Explain the reason for each of the following statements.

Metals are solid at room temperature.

_____

_____

Metals are malleable, i.e. they can be hammered into different shapes.

_____

_____

Metals conduct electricity.

_____

_____
[3]

iii) Give THREE other physical properties of metals.

1. _____

2. _____

3. _____
[3]

iv) Why do metals act as reducing agents when they react?

_____

_____
[2]

v) Using calcium as an example, give an ionic half equation to support your answer to **iv)**.

_____
[1]

C1 Characteristics of metals (cont.)

b) Metal **X** forms an ion with a charge of 2+. Metal **X** burns easily when heated in air, reacts very slowly with cold water and reacts vigorously with steam.

   i) Using **X** as the atomic symbol for the metal, write a balanced equation for the reaction between **X** and steam.

   _____

   [1]

   ii) Suggest an identity for **X**.

   _____

   [1]

c) i) Complete the following table to provide information about three metals.

Metal	Reaction when heated in air	Reaction with water or steam	Reaction with dilute hydrochloric acid
copper			
sodium	burns vigorously		
aluminium			

[8]

   ii) Write a balanced equation for EACH of the following reactions:

   the reaction between sodium and water

   _____

   aluminium reacting with oxygen

   _____

   the reaction between aluminium and hydrochloric acid.

   _____

   [6]

2 a) Some metal compounds react with dilute acids. Support this statement by writing equations to show the following reactions of metal compounds.

   i) copper(II) oxide reacting with hydrochloric acid

   _____
   [2]

   ii) the reaction between calcium carbonate and nitric acid

   _____
   [2]

   iii) magnesium hydroxide reacting with sulfuric acid

   _____
   [2]

b) i) When most metal nitrates are heated they decompose and give off one or two gases. Draw lines to match EACH of the following nitrates with the number of gases evolved when the nitrate is heated.

iron(III) nitrate		aluminium nitrate
calcium nitrate	one gas	copper(II) nitrate
sodium nitrate	two gases	potassium nitrate

[3]

ii) Write equations to show what happens when:

copper(II) nitrate is heated.

_____
[4]

sodium nitrate is heated.

_____
[4]

c) How would the action of heat on potassium carbonate differ from the action of heat on magnesium carbonate? Include the relevant equation(s).

_____

_____

_____
[3]

Total Marks _____ / 46

C2 Reactivity and extraction of metals

1 **a) i)** What is the reactivity series of metals?

_____

_____
[1]

ii) What determines how reactive a metal is?

_____
[1]

iii) Metal **Q** did not react with water or dilute hydrochloric acid, whereas metal **R** was found to react vigorously with cold water and violently with dilute hydrochloric acid. Place metals **Q**, **R**, aluminium, magnesium, iron, zinc and calcium as they would appear in the reactivity series, starting with the most reactive.

_____
[3]

b) i) The hydroxide of metal **X** was found to decompose on heating; however, the hydroxide of metal **Y** remained unchanged when it was heated. Which metal do you think is more reactive, **X** or **Y**?

_____
[1]

ii) Given that metal **X** forms an ion with a charge of 3+, use an equation to show what happened when the hydroxide of **X** was heated.

_____
[2]

iii) What would you expect to happen if metal **Y** was placed in dilute sulfuric acid?

_____
[1]

c) i) Displacement reactions can be used to determine the position of metals in the reactivity series. What is a displacement reaction?

_____

_____
[1]

94

ii) Metal **Z** was found to displace iron from iron(II) nitrate solution, but it did not react with calcium nitrate solution. Place **Z**, iron and calcium in decreasing order of reactivity.

_____

[1]

iii) Use an equation to show what happens when magnesium is placed into a solution of zinc chloride.

_____

[1]

d) Sophie placed a strip of zinc into copper(II) sulfate solution and left it for 2 hours, swirling it periodically. Her observations are shown in the diagram below.

Initially: zinc strip in copper(II) sulfate solution
After 2 hours: zinc strip in solution with pink solid

i) Identify the pink solid and give an ionic equation for its formation.

Identity of the pink solid: _____

Ionic equation: _____

[3]

ii) Why did the strip of zinc decrease in size? Support your answer with a relevant ionic equation.

Reason: _____

Ionic equation: _____

[3]

iii) What change would Sophie see in the solution?

_____

[1]

iv) Why would Sophie see the change described in **iii)** above?

_____

_____

[2]

C2 Reactivity and extraction of metals (cont.)

2 a) i) Complete the following sentence.

The extraction of a metal from its ore is a _____ process.
[1]

ii) What determines the method used to extract a metal from its ore?

_____
[1]

iii) Metal **A** appears above magnesium in the reactivity series. What method would be most suitable to extract metal **A** from its ore? Explain your answer.

Method: _____

Explanation: _____

_____
[3]

b) The diagram shows an electrolytic cell used to extract aluminium from its ore.

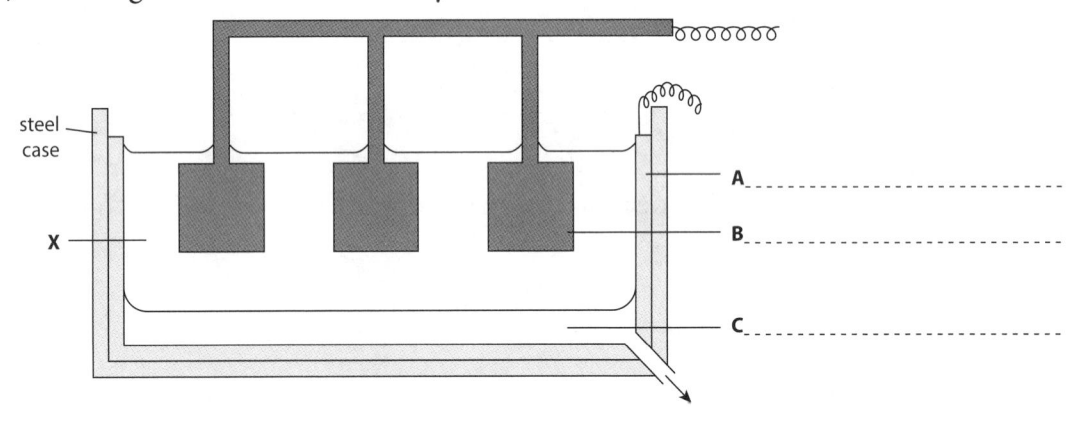

i) Label **A**, **B** and **C** in the diagram above.
[3]

ii) Name the main ore from which aluminium is extracted. _____
[1]

iii) **X** in the diagram above is composed of the ore of aluminium dissolved in molten cryolite. What is the formula of cryolite?

_____
[1]

iv) Give TWO reasons why the aluminium ore is dissolved in cryolite.

1. _____

_____

2. _____

_____

[4]

v) Write an ionic equation to show the reaction occurring at EACH electrode:

at the anode _____

at the cathode _____

[4]

3 a) Iron is extracted from its ores by heating the ores with a reducing agent in a blast furnace.

i) Name the main reducing agent in the blast furnace. _____

[1]

ii) Why is this method used to extract iron rather than electrolysis?

_____

_____

_____

[3]

iii) What are the main two ores from which iron is extracted?

1. _____ 2. _____

[2]

b) The diagram below shows a blast furnace.

C2 Reactivity and extraction of metals (cont.)

i) Other than the ores of iron, name the other two components of the charge put in at the top.

1. _____ 2. _____

[2]

ii) Label **P**, **Q** and **R** on the lines provided on the previous page. [3]

iii) Write an equation for the reaction occurring in EACH zone.

- Zone 1: _____

- Zone 2: _____

- Zone 3: _____

[5]

iv) Zone 1 has the highest temperature, what keeps it so high?

_____

[1]

v) What are the waste gases used for?

_____

[1]

vi) Silicon dioxide (SiO_2) is the main impurity in the iron ores. Explain how it is removed during the extraction process.

_____

_____

_____

_____

[4]

vii) What is the name of the iron produced in the blast furnace?

_____

[1]

Total Marks _____ / 62

C3 Uses of metals

1 **a)** Give TWO reasons for EACH of the following:

   i) Aluminium is used to make cans to store soft drinks.

      1. _____

      2. _____

                                                                                                                                [2]

   ii) Lead is used to make lead-acid batteries.

      1. _____

      2. _____

                                                                                                                                 [2]

   iii) Wrought iron is used to make ornamental ironwork.

      1. _____

      2. _____

                                                                                                                                [2]

   iv) Complete the following table to give TWO other uses for aluminium and TWO other uses for lead.

Aluminium	Lead

                                                                                                                                [4]

b) **i)** What is an alloy?

_____

                                                                                                                               [1]

C3 Uses of metals (cont.)

ii) By referring to its structure, explain why an alloy is stronger than the metal itself.

_____

_____

[2]

iii) Give the composition of magnalium. _____

[2]

iv) Other than its strength, give TWO reasons why magnalium is used in preference to aluminium in the construction of aircraft.

1. _____

2. _____

[2]

v) Name the main alloy of iron. _____

[1]

vi) What other element is usually mixed with iron to form the alloy named in **v**?

_____

[1]

vii) Name the main alloy of lead and give its composition, its main use and ONE reason why it is used in place of lead, other than its strength.

Name of alloy: _____

Composition: _____

Use: _____

Reason for use: _____

_____

[5]

Total Marks _____ / 24

C4 Impact of metals on living systems and the environment

1 a) i) What happens when a metal corrodes?

_____

_____

[2]

ii) Your parents are building a new house and they ask you if they should make the window frames out of aluminium or iron. What would you advise them to use and why?

Advice: _____ Explanation: _____

_____

_____

[3]

iii) Why is the corrosion of iron considered to be detrimental?

_____

_____

_____

[3]

b) Jamal investigated the conditions needed for iron nails to rust.

A – tap water
B – boiled water (with oil)
C – sea water
D – calcium chloride

i) What was the purpose of the cork on EACH tube?

_____

[1]

101

C4 Impact of metals on living systems and the environment (cont.)

ii) Why was the water boiled in **B**?

_____

[1]

iii) Why was oil placed on top of the water in **B**?

_____

[1]

iv) What was the role of the calcium chloride in **D**?

_____

[1]

v) Complete the following table using the words 'rusts' or 'does not rust'.

Test tube	Observations
A	
B	
C	
D	

[4]

vi) In which tube do you think Jamal saw rusting occur the fastest? _____ [1]

2 a) Give the main role of EACH of the following metal ions in living organisms.

Metal ion	Role in living organisms
iron	
magnesium	
calcium	
zinc	

[4]

102

b) i) Why is the consumption of some types of large fish a major source of ingested mercury in humans?

_____

_____

[2]

ii) Name the disease caused by the consumption of mercury and outline some of its symptoms.

Name of disease: _____

Symptoms: _____

_____

[3]

iii) Name TWO other heavy metal ions that are toxic to humans, give ONE major source of EACH in the environment and give ONE harmful effect of each.

1. Metal ion: _____

   Source: _____

   Harmful effect: _____

2. Metal ion: _____

   Source: _____

   Harmful effect: _____

[4]

iv) Disposal of solid waste containing heavy metals is a serious problem. Suggest ONE way in which this problem can be reduced.

_____

[1]

Total Marks _____ / 31

C5 Non-metals

1 a) i) In terms of atomic structure, what is a non-metal?

_____

_____
[2]

ii) Using the following, summarise the general physical properties of non-metals.

- melting and boiling points _____
- conductivity _____
- lustre _____
- hardness _____
- density _____

[5]

b) i) Why do non-metals behave as oxidising agents when they react with metals?

_____

_____
[2]

ii) Complete the following table to show how some non-metals react with calcium.

Non-metal	Equation for the reaction with calcium	Name of the product
oxygen		
hydrogen		
nitrogen		
chlorine		
sulfur		

[10]

iii) Chlorine is a powerful oxidising agent in all of its reactions. Using an equation, show it acting as an oxidising agent in its reaction with potassium iodide solution.

_____
[2]

iv) Some non-metals also react with oxygen. One of these is carbon. Write a chemical equation to summarise this reaction:

- if the oxygen supply is limited. _____

- if the oxygen supply is plentiful. _____

[3]

c) Non-metals can also act as reducing agents in some of their reactions.

i) Name THREE non-metals that can act as reducing agents.

1. _____ 2. _____ 3. _____

[3]

ii) All three non-metals named in **i)** act as reducing agents when they react with one other non-metal. Name this non-metal.

_____

[1]

2 The apparatus below can be used to prepare dry samples of both oxygen and carbon dioxide in the laboratory.

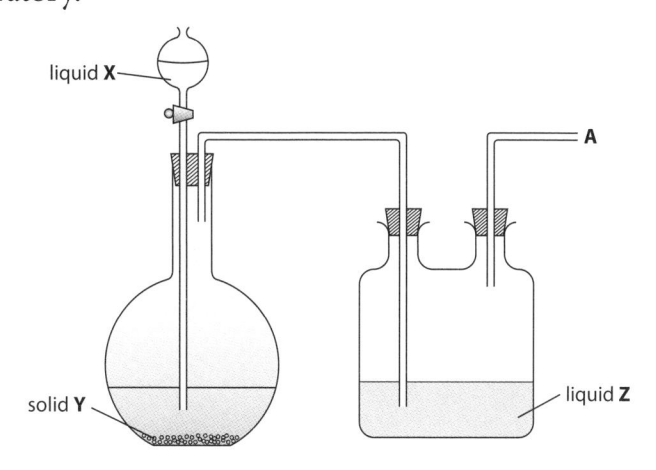

a) i) Complete the following table to give the identity of **X**, **Y** and **Z** when preparing EACH gas.

	Oxygen	Carbon dioxide
liquid **X**		
solid **Y**		
liquid **Z**		

[6]

105

C5 Non-metals (cont.)

ii) What is the function of **Z**?

_____
[1]

iii) Name another substance that could be used to perform the same function as **Z**.

_____
[1]

iv) What method would you use to collect carbon dioxide at point **A**?

_____
[1]

v) Give a reason for your answer to **iv)** above.

_____
[1]

b) Draw the apparatus you could use to prepare and collect a sample of oxygen if you did not need the sample to be dry.

[3]

c) i) Name the reagents you would use to prepare a dry sample of ammonia in the laboratory.

_____
[2]

ii) Use an equation to show how the reagents you named in **i)** react to produce ammonia.

_____

[2]

iii) Name the drying agent that should be used to dry the ammonia.

_____

[1]

iv) Explain why **Z** in the apparatus shown on page 105 could not be used to dry the ammonia.

_____

[1]

v) By what method would you collect the ammonia? _____

[1]

vi) Give a reason for your answer to **v)**.

_____

[1]

vii) Why could you not collect the ammonia over water?

_____

[1]

3 a) i) Explain why oxygen is used in welding torches.

_____

[1]

ii) Why is oxygen used in hospitals?

_____

[1]

iii) Explain why carbon dioxide is used in fire extinguishers.

_____

_____

[2]

iv) Why is solid carbon dioxide used as a refrigerant in the food industry?

_____

_____

[2]

C5 Non-metals (cont.)

b) Draw lines to match EACH of the following non-metals with one or more of its uses.

to make the heads of safety matches	carbon	as a refrigerant
to make flares	sulfur	in jewellery
to strengthen plastics	phosphorus	to make insecticides
in food packaging	chlorine	as a solid lubricant
to vulcanise rubber	nitrogen	to make the striking surface of safety matches
to treat drinking water	silicon	to make computer chips

[6]

c) Two lists follow: **A** is a list of compounds of non-metals and **B** is a list of their uses. Complete list **B** by choosing compounds from list **A**. The number of compounds required to complete list **B** is indicated by the lines provided. You may use each compound once, more than once, or not at all.

LIST A
ammonia   metal silicates   phosphoric acid   silicon dioxide   sodium carbonate
sodium chlorate[I]   sodium hydrogen carbonate   sulfur dioxide   sulfuric acid

LIST B

As a bleaching agent _____   _____

As a food preservative _____ To make ceramics _____

In the manufacture of glass _____   _____

To soften hard water _____ To manufacture fertilisers _____

_____   _____

[5]

4 a) i) Give the full name for CFCs. _____ [1]

ii) Why has the use of CFCs as aerosol propellants been banned?

_____

_____

_____

[3]

b) The carbon dioxide concentration in the atmosphere is currently increasing by about 2 parts per million each year.

i) Suggest TWO human activities that are contributing to this increase.

1. _____

2. _____

[2]

ii) This increase is contributing to the greenhouse effect. Complete the following diagram to summarise how the greenhouse effect works.

- Sun
- radiation from the Sun warms the Earth
- Earth
- Earth's atmosphere

[3]

iii) Outline some of the consequences of this gradual increase in the concentration of carbon dioxide in the atmosphere.

_____
_____
_____
_____

[4]

c) i) What is eutrophication?

_____

[1]

C5 Non-metals (cont.)

ii) What are the TWO main sources of NO_3^- and PO_4^{3-} ions that cause eutrophication?

1. _____

2. _____

[2]

iii) Outline the consequences of eutrophication to aquatic organisms.

_____

_____

_____

[3]

d) Sulfur dioxide is a major atmospheric pollutant.

i) What is the major source of sulfur dioxide in the atmosphere?

_____

[1]

ii) What does sulfur dioxide form when it dissolves in rainwater?

_____

[1]

e) Suggest THREE reasons why the disposal of solid waste containing plastics is a serious problem.

1. _____

2. _____

3. _____

[3]

5 a) Water has several unique properties. Explain the significance of EACH of the following properties of water to living organisms.

i) Water has a high heat of vaporisation.

_____

_____

[2]

ii) Water has a high specific heat capacity.

_____

_____

_____

_____
[4]

b) The diagram below illustrates another of water's unique properties. It shows a pond in winter when the air temperature was –5 °C.

(diagram showing a pond with ice on top, 0 °C just below the ice, water beneath, and 4 °C at the bottom)

i) What unique property of water is illustrated?

_____
[1]

ii) Explain why this property is important to aquatic organisms.

_____

_____

_____
[2]

c) i) Why can water dissolve a large number of substances?

_____

_____
[2]

ii) Give TWO reasons why water's solvent properties are important to living organisms.

1. _____

2. _____
[2]

iii) Give TWO reasons why the solvent properties of water can be detrimental.

1. _____

2. _____
[2]

C5 Non-metals (cont.)

d) Selena was given two samples of water and was told that one was soft and one was hard. She added 5 drops of soapy detergent to each and shook them for the same length of time. Her observations are illustrated below.

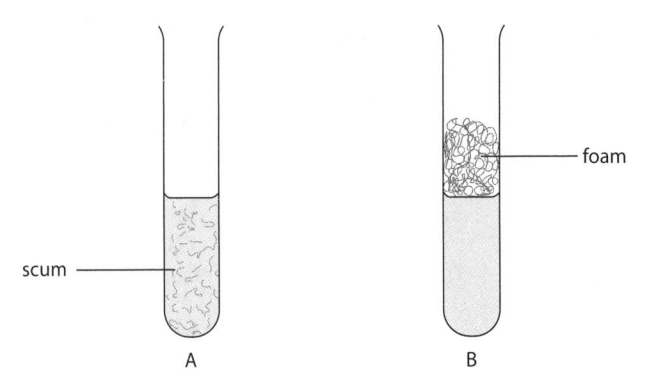

i) Which tube contained the hard water? _____

[1]

ii) What causes water to become hard?

_____

[2]

iii) Write a balanced equation to show the formation of the scum in **A**.

_____

[2]

iv) Suggest one reason why hard water is inconvenient.

_____

[1]

v) Name the TWO types of water hardness and distinguish between them.

Types: _____

Differences: _____

_____

_____

_____

[4]

6 Water can be treated in a variety of ways for domestic purposes, including chlorinating and softening.

    a) i) What effect does chlorinating have on the water?

        _____

        [1]

      ii) What happens when water is softened?

        _____

        [1]

    b) Water can be softened in a variety of ways. Outline how EACH of the following methods works to soften water and provide a relevant equation.

      i) Boiling

        Method: _____

        _____

        Equation: _____

        [2]

      ii) Addition of washing soda (sodium carbonate)

        Method: _____

        _____

        Equation: _____

        [2]

      iii) Ion exchange

        Method: _____

        _____

        Equation: _____

        [3]

7 a) i) Define 'green chemistry'.

        _____

        _____

        [1]

C5 Non-metals (cont.)

ii) Suggest THREE benefits of chemists following the principles of green chemistry.

1. _____

2. _____

3. _____

[3]

b) i) Complete EACH of the following principles of green chemistry.

Prevent _____

Design safer _____ and _____

Minimise the potential for _____

Increase energy _____

Use _____ rather than stoichiometric reagents.

Analyse in real-time to prevent _____

[7]

ii) Explain EACH of the following principles of green chemistry.

- Maximise atom economy _____

_____

- Use renewable feedstocks _____

_____

- Design for degradation _____

_____

[3]

Total Marks _____ / 139

C6 Qualitative analysis

1 a) Mario's teacher asked him to identify the cation and anion in a solid substance labelled **M**. Mario made a solution of **M** and added a few drops of sodium hydroxide solution, and saw a white precipitate that remained when he added excess sodium hydroxide solution. He then heated a sample of **M** and no change occurred, so he made a solution of **M** in dilute nitric acid and added a few drops of silver nitrate solution. A pale yellow precipitate formed, which remained when he added aqueous ammonia.

i) Identify the cation and anion in **M**.

cation: _____ anion: _____

[2]

ii) Write an ionic equation for the formation of the white precipitate.

_____

[2]

iii) Why did the precipitate remain when Mario added excess sodium hydroxide solution?

_____

[1]

iv) Write an ionic equation for the formation of the pale yellow precipitate.

_____

[1]

b) i) Shakira was given two white crystalline solids labelled **X** and **Y**, and her teacher told her that **X** was zinc nitrate and **Y** was aluminium nitrate. Describe the method Shakira would use to confirm what she was told about the identity of **X** and **Y**.

_____

_____

_____

[2]

ii) Give the results Shakira would expect.

_____

[2]

C6 Qualitative analysis (cont.)

iii) Complete the following table by inserting the observations that were made when various tests were carried out on substance **D**.

Test	Observations	Inferences
• Sodium hydroxide solution was added dropwise to a solution of **D** until in excess.	• •	• Ca^{2+}, Al^{3+}, Zn^{2+} or Pb^{2+} ions possibly present • Al^{3+}, Zn^{2+} or Pb^{2+} ions possibly present
• Aqueous ammonia was added dropwise to a solution of **D** until in excess.	• •	• Al^{3+}, Zn^{2+} or Pb^{2+} ions possibly present • Al^{3+} or Pb^{2+} ions possibly present
• A few drops of potassium iodide solution were added to a solution of **D**.	•	• Pb^{2+} ions present
• A sample of **D** was heated in a dry test tube. A glowing splint was inserted into the tube.	• •	• Nitrogen dioxide evolved • Oxygen evolved • NO_3^- ions present

[7]

iv) What reagents could you use to confirm the presence of the NO_3^- ion?

_____

[2]

v) Describe what you would expect to observe in **iv**).

_____

[2]

c) Winston conducted a series of tests on an unknown substance **K**. The tests and his observations are summarised in the following table. Fill in the table to give the inferences that Winston made from his observations. You should include the identity of any <u>gases</u> evolved, the identity of any <u>ions</u> present and relevant <u>ionic equations</u> where requested.

116

Test	Observations	Inferences
A sample of **K** was heated in a dry test tube. Pieces of moist red and blue litmus paper were held at the mouth of the tube.	• The red litmus paper turned blue. The blue litmus paper remained blue.	• •
Sodium hydroxide solution was added dropwise to a solution of **K** until in excess.	• A green precipitate formed. • The precipitate remained in excess.	• Ionic equation required:
A few drops of barium chloride solution were added to a solution of **K** followed by some dilute hydrochloric acid.	• A white precipitate formed. • The precipitate remained in the dilute acid.	• • Ionic equation required:

[8]

2 The flow diagram shows the results of various tests on substance **Q**.

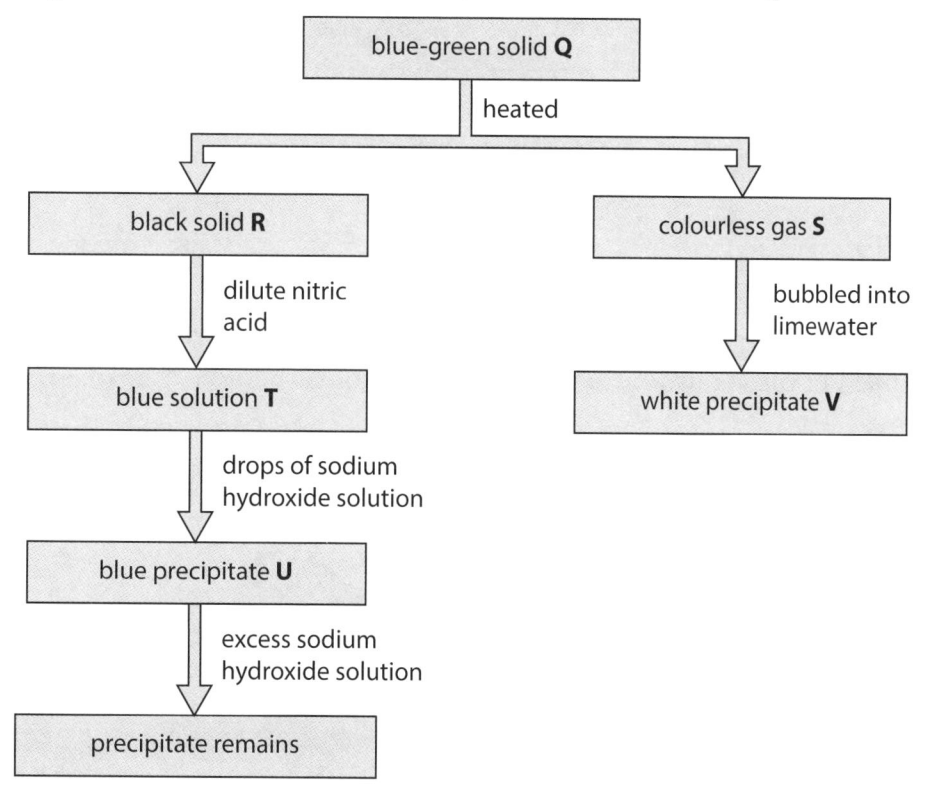

```
              blue-green solid Q
                    |
                  heated
              /           \
      black solid R      colourless gas S
           |                    |
       dilute nitric        bubbled into
          acid              limewater
           |                    |
      blue solution T     white precipitate V
           |
       drops of sodium
       hydroxide solution
           |
      blue precipitate U
           |
       excess sodium
       hydroxide solution
           |
      precipitate remains
```

117

C6 Qualitative analysis (cont.)

a) Identify substances **Q, R, S, T, U** and **V**.

Q: _____   R: _____

S: _____   T: _____

U: _____   V: _____

[6]

b) Write balanced chemical equations to summarise the following:

   i) the effect of heat on **Q**.

   _____
   [1]

   ii) the formation of precipitate **V**.

   _____
   [2]

   iii) the reaction of **R** with dilute nitric acid.

   _____
   [2]

c) Give the ionic equation for the formation of **U**.

   _____
   [2]

d) i) What difference, if any, would there have been if aqueous ammonia had been used in place of sodium hydroxide solution?

   _____

   _____
   [2]

   ii) Explain your answer to **i)**.

   _____

   _____
   [1]

e) On continued bubbling of **S** into the limewater the precipitate, **V**, dissolved forming a colourless solution. Use an equation to show why this happened.

_____

[1]

f) Describe a confirmatory test that you could carry out on the anion in **Q**.

_____

_____

[2]

3 a) Draw lines to connect EACH gas with the test used to identify it.

nitrogen dioxide	causes a glowing splint to relight
water vapour	a brown gas that turns moist blue litmus paper red
oxygen	forms white fumes with ammonia gas
hydrogen chloride	turns moist red litmus paper blue
ammonia	turns anhydrous copper(II) sulfate blue

[5]

b) An unknown gas **X** was bubbled into acidified potassium manganate(VII) solution and the solution changed from purple to colourless.

  i) Identify **X**. _____

[1]

  ii) Explain the colour change that occurred.

_____

_____

[2]

c) A piece of moist blue litmus paper was placed into another unknown gas, **Y**, and the paper turned red and then white.

  i) Identify **Y**. _____

[1]

C6 Qualitative analysis (cont.)

ii) Explain why the litmus paper turned red and then white.

_____

_____

_____ [3]

iii) Write an equation to support your answer to **ii)**.

_____ [1]

iv) Suggest another way by which the gas named in **i)** could be identified.

_____ [1]

d) Why does hydrogen cause a burning splint to make a popping sound?

_____ [1]

e) Why does water vapour change the colour of dry cobalt(II) chloride paper from pink to blue?

_____

_____ [2]

Total Marks _____ / 65

Periodic table

The Periodic Table

Period	Group I	Group II												Group III	Group IV	Group V	Group VI	Group VII	Group 0
1							1 H hydrogen 1												4 He helium 2
2	7 Li lithium 3	9 Be beryllium 4												11 B boron 5	12 C carbon 6	14 N nitrogen 7	16 O oxygen 8	19 F fluorine 9	20 Ne neon 10
3	23 Na sodium 11	24 Mg magnesium 12												27 Al aluminium 13	28 Si silicon 14	31 P phosphorus 15	32 S sulphur 16	35.5 Cl chlorine 17	40 Ar argon 18
4	39 K potassium 19	40 Ca calcium 20	45 Sc scandium 21	48 Ti titanium 22	51 V vanadium 23	52 Cr chromium 24	55 Mn manganese 25	56 Fe iron 26	59 Co cobalt 27	59 Ni nickel 28	64 Cu copper 29	65 Zn zinc 30		70 Ga gallium 31	73 Ge germanium 32	75 As arsenic 33	79 Se selenium 34	80 Br bromine 35	84 Kr krypton 36
5	85 Rb rubidium 37	88 Sr strontium 38	89 Y yttrium 39	91 Zr zirconium 40	93 Nb niobium 41	96 Mo molybdenum 42	98 Tc technetium 43	101 Ru ruthenium 44	103 Rh rhodium 45	106 Pd palladium 46	108 Ag silver 47	112 Cd cadmium 48		115 In indium 49	119 Sn tin 50	122 Sb antimony 51	128 Te tellurium 52	127 I iodine 53	131 Xe xenon 54
6	133 Cs caesium 55	137 Ba barium 56	139 La lanthanum* 57	178.5 Hf hafnium 72	181 Ta tantalum 73	184 W tungsten 74	186 Re rhenium 75	190 Os osmium 76	192 Ir iridium 77	195 Pt platinum 78	197 Au gold 79	201 Hg mercury 80		204 Tl thallium 81	207 Pb lead 82	209 Bi bismuth 83	210 Po polonium 84	210 At astatine 85	222 Rn radon 86
7	223 Fr francium 87	226 Ra radium 88	227 Ac actinium† 89																

*58–71 Lanthanum series

| 140 Ce cerium 58 | 141 Pr praseodymium 59 | 144 Nd neodymium 60 | 147 Pm promethium 61 | 150 Sm samarium 62 | 152 Eu europium 63 | 157 Gd gadolinium 64 | 159 Tb terbium 65 | 162 Dy dysprosium 66 | 165 Ho holmium 67 | 167 Er erbium 68 | 169 Tm thulium 69 | 173 Yb ytterbium 70 | 175 Lu lutetium 71 |

†90–103 Actinium series

| 232 Th thorium 90 | 231 Pa protactinium 91 | 238 U uranium 92 | 237 Np neptunium 93 | 242 Pu plutonium 94 | 243 Am americium 95 | 247 Cm curium 96 | 249 Bk berkelium 97 | 251 Cf californium 98 | 254 Es einsteinium 99 | 253 Fm fermium 100 | 256 Md mendelevium 101 | 254 No nobelium 102 | 257 Lr lawrencium 103 |

relative atomic mass

Collins

Age 16+

Full and thorough support for advanced science students

- Written by expert authors with many years' experience of teaching, examining and writing
- Encourage students to relate their learning to the world around them with Science in Context features
- Support students in monitoring their own progress with Test Yourself questions running throughout the books

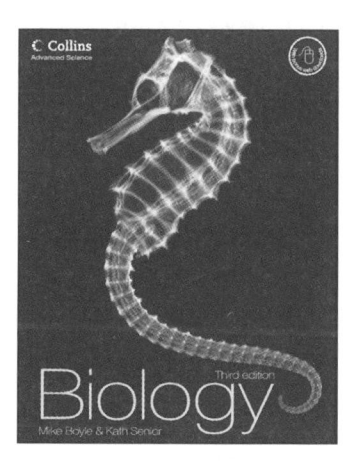

Collins Advanced Science Biology
978-0-00-726745-3

Collins Advanced Science Chemistry
978-0-00-726747-7

Collins Advanced Science Physics
978-0-00-726749-1

www.collins.co.uk/caribbeanschools

Collins

Valuable activity books for CSEC Biology, Chemistry and Physics students

- Specially written to help CSEC students maximize their exam scores
- Excellent practice for the structured questions from Paper 2
- A great aid to revision and examination practice

Collins Biology workbook for CSEC
978-0-00-811601-9
Author: Anne Tindale

Collins Chemistry workbook for CSEC
978-0-00-811602-6
Author: Anne Tindale

Collins Physics workbook for CSEC
978-0-00-811603-3
Author: Terry David

www.collins.co.uk/caribbeanschools